C-4198

CAREER EXAMINATION SERIES

OCEANSIDE LIBRARY
30 DAVISON AVENUE
OCEANSIDE, NEW YORK
PHONE (516) 766-2360

THIS IS YOUR **PASSBOOK®** FOR ...

NURSE PRACTITIONER

NLC®

NATIONAL LEARNING CORPORATION®
passbooks.com

NOV 2 5 2020

COPYRIGHT NOTICE

This book is SOLELY intended for, is sold ONLY to, and its use is RESTRICTED to individual, bona fide applicants or candidates who qualify by virtue of having seriously filed applications for appropriate license, certificate, professional and/or promotional advancement, higher school matriculation, scholarship, or other legitimate requirements of educational and/or governmental authorities.

This book is NOT intended for use, class instruction, tutoring, training, duplication, copying, reprinting, excerption, or adaptation, etc., by:

1) Other publishers
2) Proprietors and/or Instructors of «Coaching» and/or Preparatory Courses
3) Personnel and/or Training Divisions of commercial, industrial, and governmental organizations
4) Schools, colleges, or universities and/or their departments and staffs, including teachers and other personnel
5) Testing Agencies or Bureaus
6) Study groups which seek by the purchase of a single volume to copy and/or duplicate and/or adapt this material for use by the group as a whole without having purchased individual volumes for each of the members of the group
7) Et al.

Such persons would be in violation of appropriate Federal and State statutes.

PROVISION OF LICENSING AGREEMENTS. — Recognized educational, commercial, industrial, and governmental institutions and organizations, and others legitimately engaged in educational pursuits, including training, testing, and measurement activities, may address request for a licensing agreement to the copyright owners, who will determine whether, and under what conditions, including fees and charges, the materials in this book may be used them. In other words, a licensing facility exists for the legitimate use of the material in this book on other than an individual basis. However, it is asseverated and affirmed here that the material in this book CANNOT be used without the receipt of the express permission of such a licensing agreement from the Publishers. Inquiries re licensing should be addressed to the company, attention rights and permissions department.

All rights reserved, including the right of reproduction in whole or in part, in any form or by any means, electronic or mechanical, including photocopying, recording, or by any information storage and retrieval system, without permission in writing from the Publisher.

Copyright © 2020 by

National Learning Corporation

212 Michael Drive, Syosset, NY 11791
(516) 921-8888 • www.passbooks.com
E-mail: info@passbooks.com

PUBLISHED IN THE UNITED STATES OF AMERICA

PASSBOOK® SERIES

THE *PASSBOOK® SERIES* has been created to prepare applicants and candidates for the ultimate academic battlefield – the examination room.

At some time in our lives, each and every one of us may be required to take an examination – for validation, matriculation, admission, qualification, registration, certification, or licensure.

Based on the assumption that every applicant or candidate has met the basic formal educational standards, has taken the required number of courses, and read the necessary texts, the *PASSBOOK® SERIES* furnishes the one special preparation which may assure passing with confidence, instead of failing with insecurity. Examination questions – together with answers – are furnished as the basic vehicle for study so that the mysteries of the examination and its compounding difficulties may be eliminated or diminished by a sure method.

This book is meant to help you pass your examination provided that you qualify and are serious in your objective.

The entire field is reviewed through the huge store of content information which is succinctly presented through a provocative and challenging approach – the question-and-answer method.

A climate of success is established by furnishing the correct answers at the end of each test.

You soon learn to recognize types of questions, forms of questions, and patterns of questioning. You may even begin to anticipate expected outcomes.

You perceive that many questions are repeated or adapted so that you can gain acute insights, which may enable you to score many sure points.

You learn how to confront new questions, or types of questions, and to attack them confidently and work out the correct answers.

You note objectives and emphases, and recognize pitfalls and dangers, so that you may make positive educational adjustments.

Moreover, you are kept fully informed in relation to new concepts, methods, practices, and directions in the field.

You discover that you arre actually taking the examination all the time: you are preparing for the examination by "taking" an examination, not by reading extraneous and/or supererogatory textbooks.

In short, this PASSBOOK®, used directedly, should be an important factor in helping you to pass your test.

NURSE PRACTITIONER

DUTIES:
The work involves responsibility for providing direct medical care in a public health setting in collaboration with a licensed physician in accordance with written practice agreements and written practice protocols in a specific specialty area. Duties may include the diagnosis of illness and physical conditions and the performance of therapeutic and corrective measures within a specialty area of practice in collaboration with a licensed physician qualified to collaborate in the specialty involved, provided such services are performed in accordance with a written practice agreement and written practice protocols. The incumbent assesses the physical and psychological status of patients by means of interview, health history, physical examinations and diagnostic tests. Consistent with the medical protocol established, the Nurse Practitioner may evaluate test findings, make assessments and initiate appropriate actions to facilitate the implementation of preventive and/or therapeutic plans for the continuing health care needs of the patients. The work is done under the administrative supervision of a higher-level administrator. Duties must be consistent with the designated specialty's scope of practice. Does related work as required.

DISTINGUISHING FEATURES OF THE CLASS:
This is a professional position encompassing a full range of responsibilities within either the Health or Mental Health Department. The work will include physical examination, phlebotomy, injections, emergency medical care and, other nursing duties as needed, as part of the interdisciplinary team. In addition, the individual will provide counseling and education to patients in aid of prevention, treatment and rehabilitation of various types of physical or mental illness. The individual will write prescriptions (appropriate to their level of licensure) under the supervision of the medical director and departmental psychiatrists. The incumbent will perform all related duties as required.

HOW TO TAKE A TEST

I. YOU MUST PASS AN EXAMINATION

A. *WHAT EVERY CANDIDATE SHOULD KNOW*

Examination applicants often ask us for help in preparing for the written test. What can I study in advance? What kinds of questions will be asked? How will the test be given? How will the papers be graded?

As an applicant for a civil service examination, you may be wondering about some of these things. Our purpose here is to suggest effective methods of advance study and to describe civil service examinations.

Your chances for success on this examination can be increased if you know how to prepare. Those "pre-examination jitters" can be reduced if you know what to expect. You can even experience an adventure in good citizenship if you know why civil service exams are given.

B. *WHY ARE CIVIL SERVICE EXAMINATIONS GIVEN?*

Civil service examinations are important to you in two ways. As a citizen, you want public jobs filled by employees who know how to do their work. As a job seeker, you want a fair chance to compete for that job on an equal footing with other candidates. The best-known means of accomplishing this two-fold goal is the competitive examination.

Exams are widely publicized throughout the nation. They may be administered for jobs in federal, state, city, municipal, town or village governments or agencies.

Any citizen may apply, with some limitations, such as the age or residence of applicants. Your experience and education may be reviewed to see whether you meet the requirements for the particular examination. When these requirements exist, they are reasonable and applied consistently to all applicants. Thus, a competitive examination may cause you some uneasiness now, but it is your privilege and safeguard.

C. *HOW ARE CIVIL SERVICE EXAMS DEVELOPED?*

Examinations are carefully written by trained technicians who are specialists in the field known as "psychological measurement," in consultation with recognized authorities in the field of work that the test will cover. These experts recommend the subject matter areas or skills to be tested; only those knowledges or skills important to your success on the job are included. The most reliable books and source materials available are used as references. Together, the experts and technicians judge the difficulty level of the questions.

Test technicians know how to phrase questions so that the problem is clearly stated. Their ethics do not permit "trick" or "catch" questions. Questions may have been tried out on sample groups, or subjected to statistical analysis, to determine their usefulness.

Written tests are often used in combination with performance tests, ratings of training and experience, and oral interviews. All of these measures combine to form the best-known means of finding the right person for the right job.

II. HOW TO PASS THE WRITTEN TEST

A. NATURE OF THE EXAMINATION

To prepare intelligently for civil service examinations, you should know how they differ from school examinations you have taken. In school you were assigned certain definite pages to read or subjects to cover. The examination questions were quite detailed and usually emphasized memory. Civil service exams, on the other hand, try to discover your present ability to perform the duties of a position, plus your potentiality to learn these duties. In other words, a civil service exam attempts to predict how successful you will be. Questions cover such a broad area that they cannot be as minute and detailed as school exam questions.

In the public service similar kinds of work, or positions, are grouped together in one "class." This process is known as *position-classification*. All the positions in a class are paid according to the salary range for that class. One class title covers all of these positions, and they are all tested by the same examination.

B. FOUR BASIC STEPS

1) Study the announcement

How, then, can you know what subjects to study? Our best answer is: "Learn as much as possible about the class of positions for which you've applied." The exam will test the knowledge, skills and abilities needed to do the work.

Your most valuable source of information about the position you want is the official exam announcement. This announcement lists the training and experience qualifications. Check these standards and apply only if you come reasonably close to meeting them.

The brief description of the position in the examination announcement offers some clues to the subjects which will be tested. Think about the job itself. Review the duties in your mind. Can you perform them, or are there some in which you are rusty? Fill in the blank spots in your preparation.

Many jurisdictions preview the written test in the exam announcement by including a section called "Knowledge and Abilities Required," "Scope of the Examination," or some similar heading. Here you will find out specifically what fields will be tested.

2) Review your own background

Once you learn in general what the position is all about, and what you need to know to do the work, ask yourself which subjects you already know fairly well and which need improvement. You may wonder whether to concentrate on improving your strong areas or on building some background in your fields of weakness. When the announcement has specified "some knowledge" or "considerable knowledge," or has used adjectives like "beginning principles of..." or "advanced ... methods," you can get a clue as to the number and difficulty of questions to be asked in any given field. More questions, and hence broader coverage, would be included for those subjects which are more important in the work. Now weigh your strengths and weaknesses against the job requirements and prepare accordingly.

3) Determine the level of the position

Another way to tell how intensively you should prepare is to understand the level of the job for which you are applying. Is it the entering level? In other words, is this the position in which beginners in a field of work are hired? Or is it an intermediate or advanced level? Sometimes this is indicated by such words as "Junior" or "Senior" in the class title. Other jurisdictions use Roman numerals to designate the level – Clerk I, Clerk II, for example. The word "Supervisor" sometimes appears in the title. If the level is not indicated by the title, check the description of duties. Will you be working under very close supervision, or will you have responsibility for independent decisions in this work?

4) Choose appropriate study materials

Now that you know the subjects to be examined and the relative amount of each subject to be covered, you can choose suitable study materials. For beginning level jobs, or even advanced ones, if you have a pronounced weakness in some aspect of your training, read a modern, standard textbook in that field. Be sure it is up to date and has general coverage. Such books are normally available at your library, and the librarian will be glad to help you locate one. For entry-level positions, questions of appropriate difficulty are chosen – neither highly advanced questions, nor those too simple. Such questions require careful thought but not advanced training.

If the position for which you are applying is technical or advanced, you will read more advanced, specialized material. If you are already familiar with the basic principles of your field, elementary textbooks would waste your time. Concentrate on advanced textbooks and technical periodicals. Think through the concepts and review difficult problems in your field.

These are all general sources. You can get more ideas on your own initiative, following these leads. For example, training manuals and publications of the government agency which employs workers in your field can be useful, particularly for technical and professional positions. A letter or visit to the government department involved may result in more specific study suggestions, and certainly will provide you with a more definite idea of the exact nature of the position you are seeking.

III. KINDS OF TESTS

Tests are used for purposes other than measuring knowledge and ability to perform specified duties. For some positions, it is equally important to test ability to make adjustments to new situations or to profit from training. In others, basic mental abilities not dependent on information are essential. Questions which test these things may not appear as pertinent to the duties of the position as those which test for knowledge and information. Yet they are often highly important parts of a fair examination. For very general questions, it is almost impossible to help you direct your study efforts. What we can do is to point out some of the more common of these general abilities needed in public service positions and describe some typical questions.

1) General information

Broad, general information has been found useful for predicting job success in some kinds of work. This is tested in a variety of ways, from vocabulary lists to questions about current events. Basic background in some field of work, such as sociology or economics, may be sampled in a group of questions. Often these are principles which have become familiar to most persons through exposure rather than through formal training. It is difficult to advise you how to study for these questions; being alert to the world around you is our best suggestion.

2) Verbal ability

An example of an ability needed in many positions is verbal or language ability. Verbal ability is, in brief, the ability to use and understand words. Vocabulary and grammar tests are typical measures of this ability. Reading comprehension or paragraph interpretation questions are common in many kinds of civil service tests. You are given a paragraph of written material and asked to find its central meaning.

3) Numerical ability

Number skills can be tested by the familiar arithmetic problem, by checking paired lists of numbers to see which are alike and which are different, or by interpreting charts and graphs. In the latter test, a graph may be printed in the test booklet which you are asked to use as the basis for answering questions.

4) Observation

A popular test for law-enforcement positions is the observation test. A picture is shown to you for several minutes, then taken away. Questions about the picture test your ability to observe both details and larger elements.

5) Following directions

In many positions in the public service, the employee must be able to carry out written instructions dependably and accurately. You may be given a chart with several columns, each column listing a variety of information. The questions require you to carry out directions involving the information given in the chart.

6) Skills and aptitudes

Performance tests effectively measure some manual skills and aptitudes. When the skill is one in which you are trained, such as typing or shorthand, you can practice. These tests are often very much like those given in business school or high school courses. For many of the other skills and aptitudes, however, no short-time preparation can be made. Skills and abilities natural to you or that you have developed throughout your lifetime are being tested.

Many of the general questions just described provide all the data needed to answer the questions and ask you to use your reasoning ability to find the answers. Your best preparation for these tests, as well as for tests of facts and ideas, is to be at your physical and mental best. You, no doubt, have your own methods of getting into an exam-taking mood and keeping "in shape." The next section lists some ideas on this subject.

IV. KINDS OF QUESTIONS

Only rarely is the "essay" question, which you answer in narrative form, used in civil service tests. Civil service tests are usually of the short-answer type. Full instructions for answering these questions will be given to you at the examination. But in case this is your first experience with short-answer questions and separate answer sheets, here is what you need to know:

1) Multiple-choice Questions

Most popular of the short-answer questions is the "multiple choice" or "best answer" question. It can be used, for example, to test for factual knowledge, ability to solve problems or judgment in meeting situations found at work.

A multiple-choice question is normally one of three types—

- It can begin with an incomplete statement followed by several possible endings. You are to find the one ending which *best* completes the statement, although some of the others may not be entirely wrong.
- It can also be a complete statement in the form of a question which is answered by choosing one of the statements listed.
- It can be in the form of a problem – again you select the best answer.

Here is an example of a multiple-choice question with a discussion which should give you some clues as to the method for choosing the right answer:

When an employee has a complaint about his assignment, the action which will *best* help him overcome his difficulty is to
    A. discuss his difficulty with his coworkers
    B. take the problem to the head of the organization
    C. take the problem to the person who gave him the assignment
    D. say nothing to anyone about his complaint

In answering this question, you should study each of the choices to find which is best. Consider choice "A" – Certainly an employee may discuss his complaint with fellow employees, but no change or improvement can result, and the complaint remains unresolved. Choice "B" is a poor choice since the head of the organization probably does not know what assignment you have been given, and taking your problem to him is known as "going over the head" of the supervisor. The supervisor, or person who made the assignment, is the person who can clarify it or correct any injustice. Choice "C" is, therefore, correct. To say nothing, as in choice "D," is unwise. Supervisors have and interest in knowing the problems employees are facing, and the employee is seeking a solution to his problem.

2) True/False Questions

The "true/false" or "right/wrong" form of question is sometimes used. Here a complete statement is given. Your job is to decide whether the statement is right or wrong.

SAMPLE: A roaming cell-phone call to a nearby city costs less than a non-roaming call to a distant city.

This statement is wrong, or false, since roaming calls are more expensive.
This is not a complete list of all possible question forms, although most of the others are variations of these common types. You will always get complete directions for

answering questions. Be sure you understand *how* to mark your answers – ask questions until you do.

V. RECORDING YOUR ANSWERS

Computer terminals are used more and more today for many different kinds of exams.

For an examination with very few applicants, you may be told to record your answers in the test booklet itself. Separate answer sheets are much more common. If this separate answer sheet is to be scored by machine – and this is often the case – it is highly important that you mark your answers correctly in order to get credit.

An electronic scoring machine is often used in civil service offices because of the speed with which papers can be scored. Machine-scored answer sheets must be marked with a pencil, which will be given to you. This pencil has a high graphite content which responds to the electronic scoring machine. As a matter of fact, stray dots may register as answers, so do not let your pencil rest on the answer sheet while you are pondering the correct answer. Also, if your pencil lead breaks or is otherwise defective, ask for another.

Since the answer sheet will be dropped in a slot in the scoring machine, be careful not to bend the corners or get the paper crumpled.

The answer sheet normally has five vertical columns of numbers, with 30 numbers to a column. These numbers correspond to the question numbers in your test booklet. After each number, going across the page are four or five pairs of dotted lines. These short dotted lines have small letters or numbers above them. The first two pairs may also have a "T" or "F" above the letters. This indicates that the first two pairs only are to be used if the questions are of the true-false type. If the questions are multiple choice, disregard the "T" and "F" and pay attention only to the small letters or numbers.

Answer your questions in the manner of the sample that follows:

32. The largest city in the United States is
   A. Washington, D.C.
   B. New York City
   C. Chicago
   D. Detroit
   E. San Francisco

1) Choose the answer you think is best. (New York City is the largest, so "B" is correct.)
2) Find the row of dotted lines numbered the same as the question you are answering. (Find row number 32)
3) Find the pair of dotted lines corresponding to the answer. (Find the pair of lines under the mark "B.")
4) Make a solid black mark between the dotted lines.

VI. BEFORE THE TEST

Common sense will help you find procedures to follow to get ready for an examination. Too many of us, however, overlook these sensible measures. Indeed, nervousness and fatigue have been found to be the most serious reasons why applicants fail to do their best on civil service tests. Here is a list of reminders:

- Begin your preparation early – Don't wait until the last minute to go scurrying around for books and materials or to find out what the position is all about.
- Prepare continuously – An hour a night for a week is better than an all-night cram session. This has been definitely established. What is more, a night a week for a month will return better dividends than crowding your study into a shorter period of time.
- Locate the place of the exam – You have been sent a notice telling you when and where to report for the examination. If the location is in a different town or otherwise unfamiliar to you, it would be well to inquire the best route and learn something about the building.
- Relax the night before the test – Allow your mind to rest. Do not study at all that night. Plan some mild recreation or diversion; then go to bed early and get a good night's sleep.
- Get up early enough to make a leisurely trip to the place for the test – This way unforeseen events, traffic snarls, unfamiliar buildings, etc. will not upset you.
- Dress comfortably – A written test is not a fashion show. You will be known by number and not by name, so wear something comfortable.
- Leave excess paraphernalia at home – Shopping bags and odd bundles will get in your way. You need bring only the items mentioned in the official notice you received; usually everything you need is provided. Do not bring reference books to the exam. They will only confuse those last minutes and be taken away from you when in the test room.
- Arrive somewhat ahead of time – If because of transportation schedules you must get there very early, bring a newspaper or magazine to take your mind off yourself while waiting.
- Locate the examination room – When you have found the proper room, you will be directed to the seat or part of the room where you will sit. Sometimes you are given a sheet of instructions to read while you are waiting. Do not fill out any forms until you are told to do so; just read them and be prepared.
- Relax and prepare to listen to the instructions
- If you have any physical problem that may keep you from doing your best, be sure to tell the test administrator. If you are sick or in poor health, you really cannot do your best on the exam. You can come back and take the test some other time.

VII. AT THE TEST

The day of the test is here and you have the test booklet in your hand. The temptation to get going is very strong. Caution! There is more to success than knowing the right answers. You must know how to identify your papers and understand variations in the type of short-answer question used in this particular examination. Follow these suggestions for maximum results from your efforts:

1) Cooperate with the monitor

The test administrator has a duty to create a situation in which you can be as much at ease as possible. He will give instructions, tell you when to begin, check to see that you are marking your answer sheet correctly, and so on. He is not there to guard you, although he will see that your competitors do not take unfair advantage. He wants to help you do your best.

2) Listen to all instructions

Don't jump the gun! Wait until you understand all directions. In most civil service tests you get more time than you need to answer the questions. So don't be in a hurry. Read each word of instructions until you clearly understand the meaning. Study the examples, listen to all announcements and follow directions. Ask questions if you do not understand what to do.

3) Identify your papers

Civil service exams are usually identified by number only. You will be assigned a number; you must not put your name on your test papers. Be sure to copy your number correctly. Since more than one exam may be given, copy your exact examination title.

4) Plan your time

Unless you are told that a test is a "speed" or "rate of work" test, speed itself is usually not important. Time enough to answer all the questions will be provided, but this does not mean that you have all day. An overall time limit has been set. Divide the total time (in minutes) by the number of questions to determine the approximate time you have for each question.

5) Do not linger over difficult questions

If you come across a difficult question, mark it with a paper clip (useful to have along) and come back to it when you have been through the booklet. One caution if you do this – be sure to skip a number on your answer sheet as well. Check often to be sure that you have not lost your place and that you are marking in the row numbered the same as the question you are answering.

6) Read the questions

Be sure you know what the question asks! Many capable people are unsuccessful because they failed to *read* the questions correctly.

7) Answer all questions

Unless you have been instructed that a penalty will be deducted for incorrect answers, it is better to guess than to omit a question.

8) Speed tests

It is often better NOT to guess on speed tests. It has been found that on timed tests people are tempted to spend the last few seconds before time is called in marking answers at random – without even reading them – in the hope of picking up a few extra points. To discourage this practice, the instructions may warn you that your score will be "corrected" for guessing. That is, a penalty will be applied. The incorrect answers will be deducted from the correct ones, or some other penalty formula will be used.

9) Review your answers
If you finish before time is called, go back to the questions you guessed or omitted to give them further thought. Review other answers if you have time.

10) Return your test materials
If you are ready to leave before others have finished or time is called, take ALL your materials to the monitor and leave quietly. Never take any test material with you. The monitor can discover whose papers are not complete, and taking a test booklet may be grounds for disqualification.

VIII. EXAMINATION TECHNIQUES

1) Read the general instructions carefully. These are usually printed on the first page of the exam booklet. As a rule, these instructions refer to the timing of the examination; the fact that you should not start work until the signal and must stop work at a signal, etc. If there are any *special* instructions, such as a choice of questions to be answered, make sure that you note this instruction carefully.

2) When you are ready to start work on the examination, that is as soon as the signal has been given, read the instructions to each question booklet, underline any key words or phrases, such as *least, best, outline, describe* and the like. In this way you will tend to answer as requested rather than discover on reviewing your paper that you *listed without describing*, that you selected the *worst* choice rather than the *best* choice, etc.

3) If the examination is of the objective or multiple-choice type – that is, each question will also give a series of possible answers: A, B, C or D, and you are called upon to select the best answer and write the letter next to that answer on your answer paper – it is advisable to start answering each question in turn. There may be anywhere from 50 to 100 such questions in the three or four hours allotted and you can see how much time would be taken if you read through all the questions before beginning to answer any. Furthermore, if you come across a question or group of questions which you know would be difficult to answer, it would undoubtedly affect your handling of all the other questions.

4) If the examination is of the essay type and contains but a few questions, it is a moot point as to whether you should read all the questions before starting to answer any one. Of course, if you are given a choice – say five out of seven and the like – then it is essential to read all the questions so you can eliminate the two that are most difficult. If, however, you are asked to answer all the questions, there may be danger in trying to answer the easiest one first because you may find that you will spend too much time on it. The best technique is to answer the first question, then proceed to the second, etc.

5) Time your answers. Before the exam begins, write down the time it started, then add the time allowed for the examination and write down the time it must be completed, then divide the time available somewhat as follows:

- If 3-1/2 hours are allowed, that would be 210 minutes. If you have 80 objective-type questions, that would be an average of 2-1/2 minutes per question. Allow yourself no more than 2 minutes per question, or a total of 160 minutes, which will permit about 50 minutes to review.
- If for the time allotment of 210 minutes there are 7 essay questions to answer, that would average about 30 minutes a question. Give yourself only 25 minutes per question so that you have about 35 minutes to review.

6) The most important instruction is to *read each question* and make sure you know what is wanted. The second most important instruction is to *time yourself properly* so that you answer every question. The third most important instruction is to *answer every question*. Guess if you have to but include something for each question. Remember that you will receive no credit for a blank and will probably receive some credit if you write something in answer to an essay question. If you guess a letter – say "B" for a multiple-choice question – you may have guessed right. If you leave a blank as an answer to a multiple-choice question, the examiners may respect your feelings but it will not add a point to your score. Some exams may penalize you for wrong answers, so in such cases *only*, you may not want to guess unless you have some basis for your answer.

7) Suggestions
   a. Objective-type questions
      1. Examine the question booklet for proper sequence of pages and questions
      2. Read all instructions carefully
      3. Skip any question which seems too difficult; return to it after all other questions have been answered
      4. Apportion your time properly; do not spend too much time on any single question or group of questions
      5. Note and underline key words – *all, most, fewest, least, best, worst, same, opposite,* etc.
      6. Pay particular attention to negatives
      7. Note unusual option, e.g., unduly long, short, complex, different or similar in content to the body of the question
      8. Observe the use of "hedging" words – *probably, may, most likely,* etc.
      9. Make sure that your answer is put next to the same number as the question
      10. Do not second-guess unless you have good reason to believe the second answer is definitely more correct
      11. Cross out original answer if you decide another answer is more accurate; do not erase until you are ready to hand your paper in
      12. Answer all questions; guess unless instructed otherwise
      13. Leave time for review

   b. Essay questions
      1. Read each question carefully
      2. Determine exactly what is wanted. Underline key words or phrases.
      3. Decide on outline or paragraph answer

4. Include many different points and elements unless asked to develop any one or two points or elements
5. Show impartiality by giving pros and cons unless directed to select one side only
6. Make and write down any assumptions you find necessary to answer the questions
7. Watch your English, grammar, punctuation and choice of words
8. Time your answers; don't crowd material

8) Answering the essay question

Most essay questions can be answered by framing the specific response around several key words or ideas. Here are a few such key words or ideas:

M's: manpower, materials, methods, money, management
P's: purpose, program, policy, plan, procedure, practice, problems, pitfalls, personnel, public relations

   a. Six basic steps in handling problems:
1. Preliminary plan and background development
2. Collect information, data and facts
3. Analyze and interpret information, data and facts
4. Analyze and develop solutions as well as make recommendations
5. Prepare report and sell recommendations
6. Install recommendations and follow up effectiveness

   b. Pitfalls to avoid
1. *Taking things for granted* – A statement of the situation does not necessarily imply that each of the elements is necessarily true; for example, a complaint may be invalid and biased so that all that can be taken for granted is that a complaint has been registered
2. *Considering only one side of a situation* – Wherever possible, indicate several alternatives and then point out the reasons you selected the best one
3. *Failing to indicate follow up* – Whenever your answer indicates action on your part, make certain that you will take proper follow-up action to see how successful your recommendations, procedures or actions turn out to be
4. *Taking too long in answering any single question* – Remember to time your answers properly

IX. AFTER THE TEST

Scoring procedures differ in detail among civil service jurisdictions although the general principles are the same. Whether the papers are hand-scored or graded by machine we have described, they are nearly always graded by number. That is, the person who marks the paper knows only the number – never the name – of the applicant. Not until all the papers have been graded will they be matched with names. If other tests, such as training and experience or oral interview ratings have been given, scores will be combined. Different parts of the examination usually have different weights. For example, the written test might count 60 percent of the final grade, and a rating of training and experience 40 percent. In many jurisdictions, veterans will have a certain number of points added to their grades.

After the final grade has been determined, the names are placed in grade order and an eligible list is established. There are various methods for resolving ties between those who get the same final grade – probably the most common is to place first the name of the person whose application was received first. Job offers are made from the eligible list in the order the names appear on it. You will be notified of your grade and your rank as soon as all these computations have been made. This will be done as rapidly as possible.

People who are found to meet the requirements in the announcement are called "eligibles." Their names are put on a list of eligible candidates. An eligible's chances of getting a job depend on how high he stands on this list and how fast agencies are filling jobs from the list.

When a job is to be filled from a list of eligibles, the agency asks for the names of people on the list of eligibles for that job. When the civil service commission receives this request, it sends to the agency the names of the three people highest on this list. Or, if the job to be filled has specialized requirements, the office sends the agency the names of the top three persons who meet these requirements from the general list.

The appointing officer makes a choice from among the three people whose names were sent to him. If the selected person accepts the appointment, the names of the others are put back on the list to be considered for future openings.

That is the rule in hiring from all kinds of eligible lists, whether they are for typist, carpenter, chemist, or something else. For every vacancy, the appointing officer has his choice of any one of the top three eligibles on the list. This explains why the person whose name is on top of the list sometimes does not get an appointment when some of the persons lower on the list do. If the appointing officer chooses the second or third eligible, the No. 1 eligible does not get a job at once, but stays on the list until he is appointed or the list is terminated.

X. HOW TO PASS THE INTERVIEW TEST

The examination for which you applied requires an oral interview test. You have already taken the written test and you are now being called for the interview test – the final part of the formal examination.

You may think that it is not possible to prepare for an interview test and that there are no procedures to follow during an interview. Our purpose is to point out some things you can do in advance that will help you and some good rules to follow and pitfalls to avoid while you are being interviewed.

What is an interview supposed to test?

The written examination is designed to test the technical knowledge and competence of the candidate; the oral is designed to evaluate intangible qualities, not readily measured otherwise, and to establish a list showing the relative fitness of each candidate – as measured against his competitors – for the position sought. Scoring is not on the basis of "right" and "wrong," but on a sliding scale of values ranging from "not passable" to "outstanding." As a matter of fact, it is possible to achieve a relatively low score without a single "incorrect" answer because of evident weakness in the qualities being measured.

Occasionally, an examination may consist entirely of an oral test – either an individual or a group oral. In such cases, information is sought concerning the technical knowledges and abilities of the candidate, since there has been no written examination for this purpose. More commonly, however, an oral test is used to supplement a written examination.

Who conducts interviews?
The composition of oral boards varies among different jurisdictions. In nearly all, a representative of the personnel department serves as chairman. One of the members of the board may be a representative of the department in which the candidate would work. In some cases, "outside experts" are used, and, frequently, a businessman or some other representative of the general public is asked to serve. Labor and management or other special groups may be represented. The aim is to secure the services of experts in the appropriate field.

However the board is composed, it is a good idea (and not at all improper or unethical) to ascertain in advance of the interview who the members are and what groups they represent. When you are introduced to them, you will have some idea of their backgrounds and interests, and at least you will not stutter and stammer over their names.

What should be done before the interview?
While knowledge about the board members is useful and takes some of the surprise element out of the interview, there is other preparation which is more substantive. It *is* possible to prepare for an oral interview – in several ways:

1) Keep a copy of your application and review it carefully before the interview
This may be the only document before the oral board, and the starting point of the interview. Know what education and experience you have listed there, and the sequence and dates of all of it. Sometimes the board will ask you to review the highlights of your experience for them; you should not have to hem and haw doing it.

2) Study the class specification and the examination announcement
Usually, the oral board has one or both of these to guide them. The qualities, characteristics or knowledges required by the position sought are stated in these documents. They offer valuable clues as to the nature of the oral interview. For example, if the job involves supervisory responsibilities, the announcement will usually indicate that knowledge of modern supervisory methods and the qualifications of the candidate as a supervisor will be tested. If so, you can expect such questions, frequently in the form of a hypothetical situation which you are expected to solve. NEVER go into an oral without knowledge of the duties and responsibilities of the job you seek.

3) Think through each qualification required
Try to visualize the kind of questions you would ask if you were a board member. How well could you answer them? Try especially to appraise your own knowledge and background in each area, *measured against the job sought*, and identify any areas in which you are weak. Be critical and realistic – do not flatter yourself.

4) Do some general reading in areas in which you feel you may be weak
   For example, if the job involves supervision and your past experience has NOT, some general reading in supervisory methods and practices, particularly in the field of human relations, might be useful. Do NOT study agency procedures or detailed manuals. The oral board will be testing your understanding and capacity, not your memory.

5) Get a good night's sleep and watch your general health and mental attitude
   You will want a clear head at the interview. Take care of a cold or any other minor ailment, and of course, no hangovers.

What should be done on the day of the interview?
   Now comes the day of the interview itself. Give yourself plenty of time to get there. Plan to arrive somewhat ahead of the scheduled time, particularly if your appointment is in the fore part of the day. If a previous candidate fails to appear, the board might be ready for you a bit early. By early afternoon an oral board is almost invariably behind schedule if there are many candidates, and you may have to wait. Take along a book or magazine to read, or your application to review, but leave any extraneous material in the waiting room when you go in for your interview. In any event, relax and compose yourself.
   The matter of dress is important. The board is forming impressions about you – from your experience, your manners, your attitude, and your appearance. Give your personal appearance careful attention. Dress your best, but not your flashiest. Choose conservative, appropriate clothing, and be sure it is immaculate. This is a business interview, and your appearance should indicate that you regard it as such. Besides, being well groomed and properly dressed will help boost your confidence.
   Sooner or later, someone will call your name and escort you into the interview room. *This is it.* From here on you are on your own. It is too late for any more preparation. But remember, you asked for this opportunity to prove your fitness, and you are here because your request was granted.

What happens when you go in?
   The usual sequence of events will be as follows: The clerk (who is often the board stenographer) will introduce you to the chairman of the oral board, who will introduce you to the other members of the board. Acknowledge the introductions before you sit down. Do not be surprised if you find a microphone facing you or a stenotypist sitting by. Oral interviews are usually recorded in the event of an appeal or other review.
   Usually the chairman of the board will open the interview by reviewing the highlights of your education and work experience from your application – primarily for the benefit of the other members of the board, as well as to get the material into the record. Do not interrupt or comment unless there is an error or significant misinterpretation; if that is the case, do not hesitate. But do not quibble about insignificant matters. Also, he will usually ask you some question about your education, experience or your present job – partly to get you to start talking and to establish the interviewing "rapport." He may start the actual questioning, or turn it over to one of the other members. Frequently, each member undertakes the questioning on a particular area, one in which he is perhaps most competent, so you can expect each member to participate in the examination. Because time is limited, you may also expect some rather abrupt switches in the direction the questioning takes, so do not be upset by it. Normally, a board

member will not pursue a single line of questioning unless he discovers a particular strength or weakness.

After each member has participated, the chairman will usually ask whether any member has any further questions, then will ask you if you have anything you wish to add. Unless you are expecting this question, it may floor you. Worse, it may start you off on an extended, extemporaneous speech. The board is not usually seeking more information. The question is principally to offer you a last opportunity to present further qualifications or to indicate that you have nothing to add. So, if you feel that a significant qualification or characteristic has been overlooked, it is proper to point it out in a sentence or so. Do not compliment the board on the thoroughness of their examination – they have been sketchy, and you know it. If you wish, merely say, "No thank you, I have nothing further to add." This is a point where you can "talk yourself out" of a good impression or fail to present an important bit of information. Remember, *you close the interview yourself.*

The chairman will then say, "That is all, Mr. _____, thank you." Do not be startled; the interview is over, and quicker than you think. Thank him, gather your belongings and take your leave. Save your sigh of relief for the other side of the door.

How to put your best foot forward

Throughout this entire process, you may feel that the board individually and collectively is trying to pierce your defenses, seek out your hidden weaknesses and embarrass and confuse you. Actually, this is not true. They are obliged to make an appraisal of your qualifications for the job you are seeking, and they want to see you in your best light. Remember, they must interview all candidates and a non-cooperative candidate may become a failure in spite of their best efforts to bring out his qualifications. Here are 15 suggestions that will help you:

1) Be natural – Keep your attitude confident, not cocky

If you are not confident that you can do the job, do not expect the board to be. Do not apologize for your weaknesses, try to bring out your strong points. The board is interested in a positive, not negative, presentation. Cockiness will antagonize any board member and make him wonder if you are covering up a weakness by a false show of strength.

2) Get comfortable, but don't lounge or sprawl

Sit erectly but not stiffly. A careless posture may lead the board to conclude that you are careless in other things, or at least that you are not impressed by the importance of the occasion. Either conclusion is natural, even if incorrect. Do not fuss with your clothing, a pencil or an ashtray. Your hands may occasionally be useful to emphasize a point; do not let them become a point of distraction.

3) Do not wisecrack or make small talk

This is a serious situation, and your attitude should show that you consider it as such. Further, the time of the board is limited – they do not want to waste it, and neither should you.

4) Do not exaggerate your experience or abilities

In the first place, from information in the application or other interviews and sources, the board may know more about you than you think. Secondly, you probably will not get away with it. An experienced board is rather adept at spotting such a situation, so do not take the chance.

5) If you know a board member, do not make a point of it, yet do not hide it

Certainly you are not fooling him, and probably not the other members of the board. Do not try to take advantage of your acquaintanceship – it will probably do you little good.

6) Do not dominate the interview

Let the board do that. They will give you the clues – do not assume that you have to do all the talking. Realize that the board has a number of questions to ask you, and do not try to take up all the interview time by showing off your extensive knowledge of the answer to the first one.

7) Be attentive

You only have 20 minutes or so, and you should keep your attention at its sharpest throughout. When a member is addressing a problem or question to you, give him your undivided attention. Address your reply principally to him, but do not exclude the other board members.

8) Do not interrupt

A board member may be stating a problem for you to analyze. He will ask you a question when the time comes. Let him state the problem, and wait for the question.

9) Make sure you understand the question

Do not try to answer until you are sure what the question is. If it is not clear, restate it in your own words or ask the board member to clarify it for you. However, do not haggle about minor elements.

10) Reply promptly but not hastily

A common entry on oral board rating sheets is "candidate responded readily," or "candidate hesitated in replies." Respond as promptly and quickly as you can, but do not jump to a hasty, ill-considered answer.

11) Do not be peremptory in your answers

A brief answer is proper – but do not fire your answer back. That is a losing game from your point of view. The board member can probably ask questions much faster than you can answer them.

12) Do not try to create the answer you think the board member wants

He is interested in what kind of mind you have and how it works – not in playing games. Furthermore, he can usually spot this practice and will actually grade you down on it.

13) Do not switch sides in your reply merely to agree with a board member

Frequently, a member will take a contrary position merely to draw you out and to see if you are willing and able to defend your point of view. Do not start a debate, yet do not surrender a good position. If a position is worth taking, it is worth defending.

14) Do not be afraid to admit an error in judgment if you are shown to be wrong

The board knows that you are forced to reply without any opportunity for careful consideration. Your answer may be demonstrably wrong. If so, admit it and get on with the interview.

15) Do not dwell at length on your present job

The opening question may relate to your present assignment. Answer the question but do not go into an extended discussion. You are being examined for a *new* job, not your present one. As a matter of fact, try to phrase ALL your answers in terms of the job for which you are being examined.

Basis of Rating

Probably you will forget most of these "do's" and "don'ts" when you walk into the oral interview room. Even remembering them all will not ensure you a passing grade. Perhaps you did not have the qualifications in the first place. But remembering them will help you to put your best foot forward, without treading on the toes of the board members.

Rumor and popular opinion to the contrary notwithstanding, an oral board wants you to make the best appearance possible. They know you are under pressure – but they also want to see how you respond to it as a guide to what your reaction would be under the pressures of the job you seek. They will be influenced by the degree of poise you display, the personal traits you show and the manner in which you respond.

ABOUT THIS BOOK

This book contains tests divided into Examination Sections. Go through each test, answering every question in the margin. At the end of each test look at the answer key and check your answers. On the ones you got wrong, look at the right answer choice and learn. Do not fill in the answers first. Do not memorize the questions and answers, but understand the answer and principles involved. On your test, the questions will likely be different from the samples. Questions are changed and new ones added. If you understand these past questions you should have success with any changes that arise. Tests may consist of several types of questions. We have additional books on each subject should more study be advisable or necessary for you. Finally, the more you study, the better prepared you will be. This book is intended to be the last thing you study before you walk into the examination room. Prior study of relevant texts is also recommended. NLC publishes some of these in our Fundamental Series. Knowledge and good sense are important factors in passing your exam. Good luck also helps. So now study this Passbook, absorb the material contained within and take that knowledge into the examination. Then do your best to pass that exam.

EXAMINATION SECTION

EXAMINATION SECTION
TEST 1

DIRECTIONS: Each question or incomplete statement is followed by several suggested answers or completions. Select the one that BEST answers the question or completes the statement. *PRINT THE LETTER OF THE CORRECT ANSWER IN THE SPACE AT THE RIGHT.*

1. Those who are legally entitled to view a client's medical records without written consent include
    I. health care professionals who are caring for the client
    II. the client's insurer
    III. the client's son or daughter
    IV. the client's immediate nuclear family

    A. I only
    B. I and II
    C. I, II and III
    D. I, II, III and IV

2. For a nurse who provides community-based services in a senior center populated mostly by Asian-American clients, the most important preparatory skill or ability would be

    A. specialized knowledge in geriatric care
    B. mastery of how the health-care system works
    C. knowledge of the clients' culture
    D. knowledge of nutrition

3. Which of the following is an important source of insoluble dietary fiber?

    A. Whole grain foods
    B. Sweet potatoes
    C. Oats
    D. Soybeans

4. Factors that are known to contribute to heart disease include each of the following, EXCEPT

    A. sedentary lifestyle
    B. diabetes mellitus
    C. hyperlipidemia
    D. low triglycerides

5. _____ is a physiological process that affects oxygenation by limiting the amount of inspired oxygen that is delivered to the alveoli.

    A. Anemia
    B. Bradycardia
    C. Airway obstruction
    D. Fever

6. Which of the following types of data, collected during the assessment phase, would be considered subjective?

   A. The client's temperature is 98.
   B. The nurse observes that the client's face is flushed.
   C. The client states that he is nauseated and thirsty.
   D. The client's pulse is 100.

7. A nurse is designing a client teaching program that makes use of the humanistic model. The nurse's program is aimed at the client goal of

   A. becoming able to establish and maintain lifelong intimate relationships
   B. achieving her full potential
   C. gaining insight into her own behavior and being able to modify it
   D. becoming a productive member of society

8. Typically, a client's mental status is MOST effectively assessed by

   A. observing the client during the interview and examination
   B. having the client describe her mental status
   C. observing responses to a list of questions prepared in advance
   D. observing reactions to provocative questions

9. Nurses use critical thinking in the daily practice of nursing by

   A. anticipating likely medical diagnoses
   B. ensuring that there are adequate supplies on hand
   C. making conversions during medication dosage calculations
   D. setting priorities for the day

10. The oxygenation rate within body cells is regulated by the _____ gland.

    A. adrenal
    B. pineal
    C. thyroid
    D. apocrine

11. A nurse leads a group discussion on nutrition, and then asks the participants to decide on a topic of discussion for the next meeting. The nurse is representing the _____ leadership style.

    A. autocratic
    B. democratic
    C. exploitive
    D. laissez-faire

12. In order to be functional and appropriate for the situation, the nurse-client relationship must be

    A. established in an early stage by means of the nurse's statement of purpose
    B. developed from joint problem-solving work between nurse and client
    C. open-ended
    D. established by the client's willingness to accept the nurse's interventions

13. A client in a full arm cast expresses concern about preventing atrophy of the muscles in his upper arm. Assuming exercise is not contraindicated, the nurse should recommend _____ exercises.

    A. weightlifting
    B. kinetic
    C. aerobic
    D. isometric

14. An elderly client who lives at home has a history of glaucoma, for which she takes drops daily. She reports a loss of peripheral vision and an inability to adjust to darkness. Which of the following nursing diagnoses is most appropriate for her?

    A. High risk of injury related to sensory deficit
    B. High risk of injury related to impaired verbal communication
    C. High risk of injury related to lack of home safety precautions
    D. High risk for poisoning related to inadequate safeguards on medication

15. The presence of hyperemia represents the _____ stage of the inflammatory response.

    A. resolution
    B. granuloma
    C. acute vascular response
    D. chronic cellular response

16. During an assessment interview, the nurse should
    I. ask about the main problem first
    II. focus on the client, and not the signs or symptoms
    III. rely mostly on direct questions
    IV. try to avoid commentary unless it is absolutely necessary

    A. I and II
    B. I, II and IV
    C. II and III
    D. I, II, III and IV

17. Of the following clients, which would LEAST likely suffer from an imbalance in fluid, acid-base, or electrolytes?

    A. An adult with impaired cardiac function
    B. An elderly client with dementia
    C. A middle-aged client suffering from a Stage II pressure ulcer
    D. A two-year-old that has had gastroenteritis for four days

18. An overweight client with gout is discussing his diet with the nurse. During their discussion, the client should demonstrate an understanding of which foods have a high purine content. Which of the following foods would be MOST appropriate for this client?

    A. Liver
    B. Broccoli
    C. Lentils
    D. Wheat bran

19. A client has been diagnosed with terminal cancer. Shortly after the diagnosis she turns to the nurse and asks: "What should I do?" The nurse responds: "What do you think would be best for you and your family?"
The nurse has used the therapeutic communication technique of

   A. Acknowledging
   B. Refraining
   C. Metacommunication
   D. Reflecting

20. Which of the following is NOT considered a task involved in the orientation phase of the nurse-client relationship?

   A. Exploring the client's thoughts and feelings
   B. Exploring one's own feelings and fears
   C. Clarifying the problem
   D. Structuring and developing the contract

21. One of the first clinical signs of hypovolemia associated with fluid volume deficit is

   A. tachycardia
   B. edema
   C. bradycardia
   D. shortness of breath

22. A nurse is asked to obtain an arterial blood gas from a client. Of the following, the _____ artery is the LEAST appropriate site for obtaining the blood sample.

   A. femoral
   B. brachial
   C. subclavian
   D. radial

23. Parasthesia is a condition that may in itself become the etiology for other nursing diagnoses, such as

   A. knowledge deficit
   B. fibromyalgia
   C. dehydration
   D. risk for injury

24. A client diagnosed with acute pain may exhibit the defining characteristic of

   A. weight change
   B. sympathetic nervous system responses
   C. depression
   D. sleep pattern changes

25. A food label contains the following information:
   2 grams of protein
   12 grams of fat
   15.5 grams of carbohydrate
   Using the 4-4-9 method, the nurse calculates the number of total calories to be

   A. 36
   B. 97
   C. 178
   D. 256

25.____

KEY (CORRECT ANSWERS)

1.	A	11.	B
2.	C	12.	B
3.	A	13.	D
4.	D	14.	A
5.	C	15.	C
6.	C	16.	B
7.	B	17.	C
8.	A	18.	B
9.	D	19.	D
10.	C	20.	B

21.	A
22.	C
23.	D
24.	B
25.	C

TEST 2

DIRECTIONS: Each question or incomplete statement is followed by several suggested answers or completions. Select the one that BEST answers the question or completes the statement. *PRINT THE LETTER OF THE CORRECT ANSWER IN THE SPACE AT THE RIGHT.*

1. Which of the following is an example of palliative surgery?　　1.____

   A. Vascular grafting
   B. Nephrectomy
   C. Laparatomy
   D. Nerve block

2. A client has a respiratory disease that causes a chronic lack of oxygen. The nurse would need to expect and be most watchful for　　2.____

   A. peripheral edema
   B. wheezing upon exhaling
   C. flushed skin
   D. clubbing of the digits

3. In reviewing the file of a client who is scheduled for an IV pyelogram, which of the following should receive the nurse's special attention?　　3.____

   A. Hypertension
   B. Iodine allergy
   C. Diabetes mellitus
   D. Latest bowel movement

4. Which of following is NOT an advantage associated with the use of closed questions in interviewing a client?　　4.____

   A. Greater potential for revealing a client's emotional state
   B. Ease of documentation
   C. Less skill required of the interviewer
   D. More effective control of answers

5. Of the possible complications associated with blood transfusion, the most serious is　　5.____

   A. allergic reaction
   B. fever
   C. hemolysis
   D. dizziness

6. Which of the following cranial nerves is NOT assessed by evaluating the eyes and vision?　　6.____

   A. First
   B. Third
   C. Fifth
   D. Sixth

7. A 78-year-old client is brought to the emergency department after suffering vomiting and diarrhea for the last 48 hours. During the nursing assessment, the nurse observes that the client's skin is dry and can be tented, and that the client complains of an itching sensation. In developing a plan of care for the client, the most appropriate diagnosis would be

   A. risk for fall related to sensory deficit, as manifested by prolonged diarrhea and vomiting
   B. risk for fluid volume deficit related to prolonged diarrhea and vomiting
   C. risk for fluid volume excess related to prolonged diarrhea and vomiting
   D. nutrition imbalanced: less than body requirements, related to prolonged diarrhea and vomiting

8. A client who is several days post-surgery complains that none of his family has been to see him since the operation. The nurse responds: "That was your son who was here just this morning, wasn't it—The man who brought those flowers?"
   The type of therapeutic communication technique being used by the nurse is

   A. reflection
   B. focusing
   C. clarifying
   D. confrontation

9. Each of the following is a factor that commonly contributes to constipation, EXCEPT

   A. anxiety or stress
   B. decreased activity level
   C. low dietary fiber
   D. routine use of laxatives

10. The most significant contributing factor in cardiac disease is

    A. hypotension
    B. congenital heart defects
    C. alcohol abuse
    D. atherosclerosis

11. Clients are often encouraged to perform deep breathing exercises after surgery, in order to

    A. counteract respiratory acidosis
    B. increase cardiac output
    C. expand residual volume
    D. increase blood volume

12. Which of the following hormones acts to preserve sodium ions in the body's cells?

    A. Thyrocalcitonin
    B. Androstenone
    C. Cortisone
    D. Aldosterone

13. Which of the following is NOT an example of tertiary care?

    A. Neurosurgery
    B. Promoting workplace safety
    C. Hospice care
    D. Burn care

14. A client has died. Because proper handling of a client's body after death is an important intervention, the nurse should

    A. cover the client completely with a sheet before family members are allowed into the room
    B. apply makeup, jewelry, and any other accessories that the person wore in life before allowing the family into the room
    C. make sure the body looks as clean and natural as possible
    D. leave the body exactly as it was at the moment of death until a physician has arrived to formalize the death pronouncement

15. The nurse is meeting a new client. Which of the following would be MOST effective in initiating the nurse-client relationship?

    A. Asking the client why she was brought to the hospital.
    B. Explaining the purpose of and plan for the relationship
    C. Waiting until the client indicates a readiness to establish a relationship.
    D. Describing her family background, and then asking the client to do the same.

16. Together, a nurse and a client devise a nursing care plan with one goal being the maintenance of adequate fluid volume. The achievement of this goal can most accurately be measured by

    A. auscultation for heart and vascular sounds
    B. palpating for skin turgor, pulse, and heart rhythm
    C. monitoring bowel elimination patterns
    D. monitoring serum glucose

17. Nursing care and treatment of pressure sores is executed under each of the following general guidelines or recommended practices, EXCEPT the

    A. use of alcohol to clean and dress sores
    B. frequent repositioning of the client
    C. tissue sampling from infected sores
    D. application of cornstarch to the bedsheet

18. Clients should be screened for tuberculosis every

    A. six months
    B. year
    C. 2 years
    D. 5 years

19. Which of the following represents a primary source of data during the assessment phase of the nursing process?

    A. The client states that she has been suffering from intermittent dizzy spells.
    B. The client's spouse says the she has seemed severely fatigued lately.
    C. The client's chart documents a history of epilepsy.
    D. The client's temperature is 99° F.

20. A client with a broken left hand is awaiting an X-ray. Which of the following nonpharmacological interventions is most appropriate to help the client reduce pain prior to the procedure?

    A. Applying ice directly over the break
    B. Turning of the lights and eliminating other sensory stimuli
    C. Applying ice to the left elbow
    D. Applying warmth directly over the break

21. A nurse is planning an educational program on the detection of cancer, to be presented at a community clinic. Which of the following elements is LEAST likely to help address the various learning styles of the clients?

    A. A lecture
    B. Specific examples/case studies
    C. Audiovisuals
    D. Collaborative activities

22. Which of the following is an example of an outcome evaluation?

    A. A review of nursing documentation for compliance with institutional standards
    B. A survey to analyze staffing patterns
    C. Checking a client's temperature before administering a new medication
    D. An audit that records the number of postoperative infections

23. Which of the following tasks is part of the working phase of the nurse-client relationship?

    A. Identifying client problems
    B. Establishing trust
    C. Developing a plan for interaction
    D. Reviewing progress and attainment of goals

24. Which of the following is the body's mechanism for preventing pressure sores?

    A. third-space movement
    B. ischemia
    C. vasoconstriction
    D. vasodilation/hyperemia

25. If a client is hearing-impaired, the nurse should establish and maintain therapeutic communication by

    A. learning sign language
    B. using an inteipreter
    C. using simple sentences
    D. orienting the client to sounds in the environment

KEY (CORRECT ANSWERS)

1. D
2. D
3. B
4. A
5. C

6. A
7. B
8. C
9. A
10. D

11. A
12. D
13. B
14. C
15. A

16. B
17. A
18. C
19. A
20. C

21. A
22. D
23. A
24. D
25. C

TEST 3

DIRECTIONS: Each question or incomplete statement is followed by several suggested answers or completions. Select the one that BEST answers the question or completes the statement. *PRINT THE LETTER OF THE CORRECT ANSWER IN THE SPACE AT THE RIGHT.*

1. A nurse asks a client: "What kind of abdominal pain are you feeling today?" What kind of assessment is being performed?   1.____

    A. Time-lapsed
    B. Problem-focused
    C. Initial
    D. Emergency

2. A client has been placed on a high-fiber diet. Which of the following foods would be LEAST likely to contribute to the diet?   2.____

    A. Green peppers
    B. Cheese
    C. Apples
    D. Wheat bread

3. A "chronic" illness is generally defined as one that lasts for more than   3.____

    A. six weeks
    B. 3 months
    C. 6 months
    D. 1 year

4. Which of the following is NOT a sign of cardiac arrest?   4.____

    A. Crepitations auscultated in lungs
    B. No carotid pulse
    C. Dilated pupils
    D. Apnea

5. For a client who is admitted with gastrointestinal bleeding, one of the earliest and most important blood tests will be the   5.____

    A. complete blood count
    B. Coombs test
    C. arterial blood gases
    D. lipid panel

6. A nursing care plan for a client with a diagnosis of chronic pain related to compression of the spinal nerves involves two goals: the client will achieve a sense of pain relief within 1 month, and the client will perform self-care measures with less discomfort on self-report within 14 days. Which of the following would be an appropriate evaluation of the effectiveness of the care plan?   6.____

    A. Observing whether client has returned to social activities within 14 days
    B. Observing the client's facial expression in response to the application of localized heat
    C. Observing client's freedom of movement and facial expressions for signs of discomfort
    D. Asking if client's pain has remained localized within initially described boundaries

11

7. In planning client teaching, the nurse's instruction should be most significantly guided by the knowledge that

   A. each client has unique learning needs
   B. a client's cultural background is the most important factor in determining his or her learning needs
   C. all clients share the same basic learning needs
   D. a client's learning needs are most strongly correlated with his or her life stage

8. One of the goals of a nursing care plan is for a client to return to within 10 percent of his ideal body weight. Each of the following would be an appropriate outcome to go along with this goal, EXCEPT

   A. the client loses 2 kg per week
   B. the client gains 2 kg per week
   C. the client verbalizes positive feelings about weight loss or gain
   D. the client selects appropriate foods to facilitate weight gain or loss

9. A client is recovering from a stroke and is aphasic. To establish and maintain therapeutic communication with this client, the nurse should

   A. ask brief questions that require "yes" or "no" answers
   B. be sure to provide some introductory language before each procedure or activity
   C. make as many decisions as feasible for the client, to avoid agitating her
   D. speak very slowly and enunciate clearly

10. A client is semiconscious and likely to obstruct her own airway with her tongue. If the client requires respiratory intubation and there are no contraindications, a(n) _____ tube should be used.

    A. oropharyngeal
    B. endotracheal
    C. tracheostomy
    D. nasopharyngeal

11. A nurse asks a client to close his eyes, and then places a spoon in his palm and asks the client to identify the object. Which evaluation is the nurse performing?

    A. Stereognosis
    B. Tactile spatial acuity
    C. Texture discrimination
    D. Proprioception

12. A 38-year-old woman has a diagnosis of nocturia, probably caused by pregnancy. The nurse should recommend that the client

    A. restrict fluid intake in evening and nighttime hours
    B. consult a urologist
    C. make use of a nighttime alarm to alert her when an episode is occurring
    D. avoid eating citrus fruits

13. A doctor has ordered that a client take 6 ml of a medication in solution. The nurse's equipment is marked for fluid ounces (oz). How many ounces should the nurse administer?

    A. 0.2
    B. 0.8
    C. 1.2
    D. 2.4

14. A nurse is assessing a new client for possible impairment of verbal communication. Each of the following should be a component of the assessment, EXCEPT

    A. vision
    B. level of education
    C. hearing
    D. cognitive function

15. While recovering from surgery, a client avoids eye contact with the attending nurse, both while being cared for and when speaking. This is most likely a sign that the client is feeling

    A. ashamed
    B. fearful
    C. angry
    D. weak and defenseless

16. In nurse-client communication, which of the following variables is an emotional/psychological barrier to effective reception of a message?

    A. Using one's personal experience or frame of reference in interpreting
    B. Lack of context
    C. Distorting the message to comply with one's own expectations
    D. Insufficient vocabulary

17. Total parenteral nutrition (TPN) is usually contraindicated in clients whose gastrointestinal tracts are functional within _____ following an illness, surgery, or trauma.

    A. 24 hours
    B. 3 to 5 days
    C. 7 to 10 days
    D. 1 month

18. A client is undergoing oxygen therapy. The nurse can most effectively evaluate the effectiveness of this therapy by observing changes in

    A. blood volume
    B. serum electrolyte values
    C. arterial blood gases
    D. respiration

19. Which of the following nursing skills is most likely to be required during the pre-interaction phase of the nurse-client relationship?

    A. Analyzing one's one strengths and limitations
    B. Exploring relevant stressors
    C. Overcoming resistance behaviors
    D. Establishing trust

20. A nurse is instructed to give an IM injection into the ventrogluteal muscle. Each of the following would be a landmark used for this procedure, EXCEPT the

    A. lateral femoral condyle
    B. iliac crest
    C. greater trochanter
    D. anterior superior iliac spine

21. A nurse observes that a client's stool is green, loose, and has a strong odor. Based on this assessment, the next step of the nursing process that should be implemented is

    A. evaluating
    B. assessing
    C. implementing
    D. diagnosing

22. The main consequence of repeated vomiting is

    A. fluid and electrolyte loss
    B. dental caries
    C. metabolic alkalosis
    D. sleep disorder

23. Of the following medical conditions, which is most appropriate for the use of a nursing critical pathway?

    A. Knee replacement surgery
    B. Polyuria associated with pregnancy
    C. Viral infection acquired during travel
    D. Ear blockage by impacted cerumen

24. Coping or defense mechanisms that are used by clients include each of the following EXCEPT

    A. projection   B. reinvention
    C. compensation   D. denial

25. A client who recently suffered a herniated spinal disc complains of pain in her foot. During the nursing assessment, the nurse discovers no problems with the foot. The client's pain is best described as

    A. referred   B. neuropathic
    C. phantom   D. somatic

KEY (CORRECT ANSWERS)

1.	B	11.	A
2.	B	12.	A
3.	B	13.	A
4.	A	14.	B
5.	A	15.	D
6.	C	16.	C
7.	A	17.	C
8.	C	18.	C
9.	A	19.	A
10.	A	20.	A

21. D
22. A
23. A
24. B
25. A

EXAMINATION SECTION
TEST 1

DIRECTIONS: Each question or incomplete statement is followed by several suggested answers or completions. Select the one that BEST answers the question or completes the statement. *PRINT THE LETTER OF THE CORRECT ANSWER IN THE SPACE AT THE RIGHT.*

1. Which of the following is NOT a characteristic of the nursing care plan?

    A. It focuses on the present, rather than the future.
    B. It is based on identifiable health and nursing problems.
    C. It is a product of a deliberate systematic process.
    D. Its focus is holistic, rather than localized.

2. What method of wound debridement is generally least damaging?

    A. Scissors
    B. Chemical
    C. Wet to dry dressings
    D. Mechanical

3. Which of the following types of medications is LEAST likely to increase a client's risk of falling?

    A. antidepressants
    B. laxatives
    C. antibiotics
    D. diuretics

4. For most adults, healthy elimination patterns usually require a fluid intake of at least _____ ml daily.

    A. 750-1250
    B. 1500-2200
    C. 2000-3000
    D. 3500-5000

5. Which of the following is NOT a clinical guideline for assessing possible decubitus sites on a partially immobilized client?

    A. Avoiding incandescent light
    B. Inspecting for abrasions/excoriations
    C. Palpating skin temperature over pressure areas
    D. Elevating room temperature during assessment

6. During the assessment phase, a nurse will need to validate data when
    I. the data lack objectivity
    II. there is a discrepancy between what the client is saying and what the nurse is observing
    III. the data are not relevant to the client's presenting problem

    A. I only   B. I and II   C. II only   D. I, II and III

7. Following a mastectomy, a client says to a nurse: "The scar isn't as bad as I thought it was going to be." The client's eyes tear up and she looks anxious when she says this. Her message is an example of

   A. the Hawthorne effect
   B. congruence
   C. understatement
   D. metacommunication

8. In the _____ stage of the nursing process, the nurse ensures that the client is receiving the prescribed therapy at the appropriate times.

   A. evaluating
   B. diagnosing
   C. assessing
   D. planning/implementing

9. Among the following, the example that best represents "passive immunity" is

   A. a newborn receiving breast milk from his mother
   B. an infected person taking antibiotic medication
   C. an infected person producing antibodies
   D. a person receiving an influenza vaccine

10. The most common form of dementia is

    A. dementia due to Parkinson's disease
    B. AIDS dementia complex
    C. vascular dementia
    D. Alzheimer's disease

11. Which of the following positions puts the client at greatest risk for aspirating secretions?

    A. Sim's
    B. Fowler's
    C. Lateral
    D. Supine

12. The main factor that differentiates chronic pain from acute pain is that a client who is experiencing chronic pain is more likely to have

    A. a tissue injury
    B. a rapid pulse
    C. warm, dry skin
    D. dilated pupils

13. A client is refusing a blood transfusion because she says the procedure goes against her religious beliefs. The most appropriate action for the nurse to take is to

    A. notify a close family member who might persuade the client to undergo the procedure
    B. seek a court order compelling the client to submit to the procedure
    C. provide all the information the client needs to make an informed decision
    D. ask questions that probe the client's rationale, such as: "Do you think God would want for you to bleed to death?"

14. Which of the following nursing notes is an example of subjective data?

    A. Pulse is erratic
    B. Client's gait is unsteady
    C. Client's left hand is cool to the touch
    D. Client complains of headache

15. Each of the following would be an appropriate nursing intervention for a client with a chest drainage system, EXCEPT

    A. Placing the client in the Sim's position
    B. Monitoring the integrity of the drainage system
    C. Maintaining the water seal area of the unit
    D. Using clamps when appropriate

16. Which of the following is characteristic of the chronic cellular response phase of the inflammatory response?

    A. erythema
    B. hyperemia
    C. granuloma
    D. margination

17. When a nurse is preparing to teach a client, it is most useful for the nurse to know the client's

    A. educational background
    B. personal preferences
    C. family status
    D. developmental stage

18. For a client with sensory deficit, a nurse can appropriately increase environmental stimuli by

    A. using the television to provide intermittent auditory and visual stimuli
    B. installing a nightlight near the client's bed
    C. freeing the room of unnecessary clutter
    D. establishing a mealtime routine

19. A nurse informs a client: "Your arterial blood gases will be evaluated at seven p.m. tonight." Later, the client seems surprised and upset by the arterial blood draw. In informing the client about the procedure, the nurse's words probably required a greater measure of

    A. clarity
    B. simplicity
    C. timing
    D. tact

20. Which of the following is a term that denotes an isotonic gain of water and electrolytes?   20._____

    A. Dehydration
    B. Superhydration
    C. Fluid volume deficit
    D. Fluid volume excess

21. Of following clients, the one most likely to suffer a vitamin B deficiency would be the one who   21._____

    A. is on a low-residue diet
    B. abuses alcohol
    C. is pregnant
    D. does not regularly exercise

22. A nurse is attempting to establish a therapeutic environment for a confused elderly client. Of the following, the nurse should place the highest priority on   22._____

    A. a fixed routine
    B. supportive group interactions
    C. a trusting relationship
    D. a variety of activities

23. A client with a respiratory disease is only able to breathe when he is in an upright or standing position. In charting the client's condition, the nurse would use the medical term_____ to describe this condition.   23._____

    A. orthopnea
    B. tachypnea
    C. bradypnea
    D. apnea

24. A client is to have oxygen delivered in concentrations between 60 and 70 percent, at an average flow of 6.5 liters per minute. What type of mask should be used?   24._____

    A. Simple face mask
    B. Nonrebreather
    C. Partial rebreather
    D. Venturi

25. An elderly client was admitted to the emergency room three hours ago and has been hydrated with half-normal saline. During a subsequent assessment, the nurse observes a rapid pulse and shortness of breath. The nurse suspects that the client is showing signs of   25._____

    A. hypovolemia
    B. hypernatremia
    C. hypokalemia
    D. hypervolemia

KEY (CORRECT ANSWERS)

1.	A	11.	D
2.	B	12.	C
3.	C	13.	C
4.	C	14.	D
5.	D	15.	A
6.	B	16.	D
7.	D	17.	D
8.	D	18.	D
9.	A	19.	B
10.	D	20.	D

21. B
22. C
23. A
24. C
25. D

TEST 2

DIRECTIONS: Each question or incomplete statement is followed by several suggested answers or completions. Select the one that BEST answers the question or completes the statement. *PRINT THE LETTER OF THE CORRECT ANSWER IN THE SPACE AT THE RIGHT.*

1. In order to keep nurse-client communications therapeutic, the nurse should

    A. continue pushing the client toward some insights into his or her health behaviors
    B. make sure the conversation lasts for as long as the client wants to remain engaged
    C. make sure conversations remain goal-centered
    D. include prescriptive and directive language in the conversation

1.____

2. Which of the following body fluids is NOT associated with bloodborne pathogens?

    A. Vaginal secretions
    B. Pleural fluid
    C. Cerebrospinal fluid
    D. Nasal secretions

2.____

3. During an assessment interview, the nurse should use _____ questions to validate or clarify information.

    A. rhetorical
    B. direct
    C. open-ended
    D. reflective

3.____

4. A typical nursing intervention aimed at promoting the transport of oxygen and carbon dioxide is to

    A. reduce stress, in order to optimize cardiac output
    B. perform percussion, vibration, and postural drainage
    C. encourage coughing or deep breathing
    D. increase the amount of dietary fiber

4.____

5. A nurse is trying to help an elderly client regain urinary continence. Which of the following interventions would NOT be helpful?

    A. Teaching Kegel exercises
    B. Prompted voiding
    C. Restricting fluid intake
    D. Habit training/toilet scheduling

5.____

6. Kegel exercises are designed to strengthen the pubococcygeal muscle. Benefits associated with this exercise include
    I. reduced menstrual pain
    II. preparation for normal vaginal childbirth
    III. increased sexual gratification
    IV. improved urinary continence

    A. I and II
    C. III and IV
    B. I, III and IV
    D. I, II, III and IV

6.____

22

7. Each of the following is a risk factor that contributes to the formation of pressure ulcers, EXCEPT

   A. incontinence
   B. low blood protein
   C. inactivity
   D. lowered body temperature

8. Which of the following nursing activities poses the greatest risk for stress or injury to the nurse's back?

   A. Turning a client in bed
   B. Transferring a client in or out of bed
   C. Helping a client stand from a sitting position
   D. Helping a client walk

9. A nurse learns that a client does not appear to completely understand the risks of the surgery for which he is scheduled tomorrow. The nurse should notify the

   A. client's family
   B. surgical unit
   C. institution's administrative office
   D. surgeon

10. Client _____ behaviors are often encountered during the introductory phase of the nurse-client relationship, and may be due to difficulty in acknowledging the need for help, fear of exposing and facing feelings, and anxiety about changing behavior patterns.

    A. affiliative
    B. hostile
    C. resistive
    D. dependent

11. A nurse is establishing a therapeutic relationship with a client whose cultural background is vastly different from his own. It is important for the nurse, in establishing this relationship, to

    A. not mention the difference to the client, but remain aware of it throughout interactions
    B. ignore or minimize the difference
    C. wait for the client to mention the difference
    D. acknowledge the difference forthrightly

12. Together, the nurse and client devise a nursing care plan that includes the goal of maintaining fluid and electrolyte balances within normal limits. Each of the following would be an evaluation that could help measure outcomes for this goal, EXCEPT

    A. monitoring bowel elimination patterns
    B. weighing the client
    C. palpation for edema and skin breakdown
    D. monitoring vital signs for tachycardia, dysrhythmias, hypertension, and dyspnea

13. Under the nurse's teaching, a client is learning how to use crutches after a knee operation. The nurse should instruct the client to do each of the following, EXCEPT to

    A. adjust the length of the crutches frequently and independently, until they are comfortable
    B. regularly inspect the crutch tips
    C. remain as erect as possible when using them
    D. use the arms, and not the armpit pads, to support weight

14. A nurse is teaching a 24-year-old client with insulin-dependent diabetes to manage his diet, sugars, and insulin regimen. The client will most likely be interested in learning this information from the nurse if the nurse

    A. makes the client sufficiently aware that the disease can be life-threatening
    B. reminds the client that he has several family members who rely on him to remain healthy and able-bodied
    C. is able to fully communicate the future implications of uncontrolled diabetes
    D. is able to relate the need for control of certain factors in the client's present-day life

15. A client reports to the emergency department complaining of angina and shortness of breath. Before performing a physical assessment of this client, the nurse obtains a history. Which of the following data will be relevant for this client?

    A. History of diabetes or smoking
    B. History of atrial fibrillation
    C. History of taking dietary supplements
    D. Allergy history

16. Dorothea Orem's nursing model is based on the principle that

    A. the best people to care for a client are his or her family, with help from medical professionals
    B. all clients wish to care for themselves
    C. the nurse acts as a gatekeeper, both for information and therapeutic care
    D. the client is an interrelated set of systems: biological, psychological, and social

17. A nurse who is preparing a client for a sigmoidoscopy would

    A. explain to the client that she will have to swallow a chalky substance before the examination
    B. explain the client that no fluids can be ingested within 24 hours prior to the examination
    C. administer an enema on the morning of the examination
    D. collect a stool specimen from the client

18. A nurse is preparing a client for a series of diagnostic tests. When explaining the tests to the client, the nurse should

    A. provide specific and detailed information about each test involved in the series
    B. provide minimal answers to client questions if the client appears anxious
    C. provide enough information to help the client understand the procedures, but not so much as to overwhelm her
    D. wait until just prior to each test, in order to postpone unnecessary anxiety

19. The leading cause of injury in older adults is   19._____

   A. medication dosage error
   B. automobile accidents
   C. exposure/hypothermia
   D. falling

20. A client has end stage renal disease. Upon reporting for his shift, the nurse learns that   20._____
    the client's vital signs have been dropping throughout the day. The nurse enters the client's room and sees that her dentures and bed linens are dirty, and her hair is unkempt. His plan for intervention should include

   A. recommending that the client remove her dentures
   B. asking the client what she needs to be more comfortable
   C. telling the client that her hair must be washed
   D. asking the client if she can get herself out of bed so that the linens can be changed

21. The nurse who wants to assess a client's temperature at its highest daily level should   21._____
    take temperature readings at

   A. 8 p.m. and midnight
   B. 3 p.m. and 9 p.m.
   C. noon and 5 p.m.
   D. 3 a.m. and 7 a.m.

22. A client has been placed on a soft diet. Which of the following foods would NOT be   22._____
    allowed?

   A. Tofu
   B. Oatmeal
   C. Raisins
   D. Yogurt

23. A client's medication order reads "Keflex 250 mg po." The drug is available as Keflex 125   23._____
    mg/ml. The nurse should give _____ ml.

   A. 2
   B. 12
   C. 20
   D. 45

24. A nurse who, throughout every facet of his work, shows that he is answerable to himself   24._____
    and those in authority is demonstrating that he is

   A. accountable
   B. responsible
   C. ethical
   D. beneficent

25. A nurse finds a client's distraught mother in the client's room, long after visiting hours have been ended. The client is asleep. The nurse tells the mother in a calm, patient voice that she will have to go home for the night. The mother responds, but the nurse does not attend to her response because he is thinking that the institution's policy, in this case, is not helpful to the client or his family. This kind of distraction in communication is known as

    A. scapegoating
    B. intrapersonal communication
    C. derailing
    D. cross-talk

25._____

KEY (CORRECT ANSWERS)

1.	C	11.	D
2.	D	12.	A
3.	B	13.	A
4.	A	14.	D
5.	C	15.	A
6.	C	16.	B
7.	D	17.	C
8.	B	18.	C
9.	D	19.	D
10.	C	20.	B

21. A
22. C
23. A
24. A
25. B

TEST 3

DIRECTIONS: Each question or incomplete statement is followed by several suggested answers or completions. Select the one that BEST answers the question or completes the statement. *PRINT THE LETTER OF THE CORRECT ANSWER IN THE SPACE AT THE RIGHT.*

1. A therapeutic relationship
   I. involves an emotional commitment
   II. is goal-directed
   III. is planned
   IV. focuses on client needs

   A. I and II
   B. I, II and III
   C. II, III and IV
   D. I, II, III and IV

2. A brachial pulse is taken typically to

   A. obtain the most accurate reading possible
   B. measure blood pressure
   C. to calculate resting heart rate
   D. determine cerebral circulation

3. The most important difference between a nursing diagnosis and a medical diagnosis is that

   A. medical diagnoses are evidence-based, while nursing diagnoses are anecdotal
   B. nurses are not allowed to engage in medical diagnosis
   C. nursing diagnoses focus on human responses to stimuli, while medical diagnoses focus on the disease process.
   D. nursing diagnoses focus on health promotion, while medical diagnoses focus on treatment

4. A client's wound is draining thick yellow material. Which of the following descriptions would be LEAST appropriate in describing the wound?

   A. Purulent
   B. Pyogenic
   C. Serous
   D. Suppurative

5. A client has been admitted to the emergency room complaining of a headache and weakness. The nurse observes that she appears confused and has warm, flushed skin. Her vital signs are as follows: T 101.8; HR 124; R 22; and BP 128/90. A blood gas sample was taken on room air, with the following results: pH 7.35; pCO_2 58; pO_2 70; HCO_3 23. The client is at risk for

   A. metabolic acidosis
   B. metabolic alkalosis
   C. respiratory acidosis
   D. respiratory alkalosis

6. A client is referred to a nurse by a local women's shelter, where she has fled a violent marriage. The client tells the nurse she is having trouble deciding whether to continue the relationship with her husband. The most appropriate nursing diagnosis for this client is

   A. risk for injury
   B. readiness for enhanced spiritual well-being
   C. decisional conflict
   D. energy field disturbance

7. Which of the following is LEAST likely to be a site for a skinfold test during a nursing assessment?

   A. Subiliac
   B. Triceps
   C. Subscapula
   D. Thigh

8. Weight loss, described as "severe" once it exceeds _____ percent, is one of the clinical signs of fluid volume deficit.

   A. 5
   B. 8
   C. 12
   D. 20

9. Which of the following is NOT a fluid/electrolyte condition that is typically caused by stress?

   A. Hypervolemia
   B. Reduced cellular metabolism
   C. Sodium retention
   D. Water retention

10. When evaluating a family's coping resources, a nurse should consider the

    A. structure of the family
    B. availability of support
    C. individual roles of family members
    D. family's preventive health practices

11. Which of the following is MOST likely to be a therapeutic communication technique when used by a nurse?

    A. Challenging
    B. Advising
    C. Disagreeing
    D. Restating

12. A client who has recently broken his arm complains of a dull, generalized pain along his forearm. This type of pain is best described as

    A. somatic   B. cutaneous
    C. phantom   D. visceral

13. A nurse is teaching a client about a low-cholesterol diet. Which of the following activities is MOST likely to facilitate retention? 13.____

    A. breaking down the lesson into individual units that are followed by quizzes
    B. under the nurse's supervision, having the client develop a weekly menu by selecting foods
    C. assigning reading and computer-aided activities
    D. using visual aids with bold line drawings

14. Which of the following nursing interventions is MOST appropriate for a client with a urinary tract infection? 14.____

    A. Facilitate access to toilet
    B. Encourage fluid intake
    C. Decrease calcium intake
    D. Teach Kegel exercises

15. With a completely or partially immobilized client, many nursing interventions for the respiratory system are aimed at promoting expansion of the chest and lungs. Of the following, the most effective intervention for this purpose is 15.____

    A. isometric exercises
    B. physiotherapy
    C. frequent position changes
    D. aerobic exercise

16. Together, a nurse and client are working on a plan to reduce the client's health risk factors. Which of the following interventions would be LEAST effective in assisting the client? 16.____

    A. Asking the client identify three goals for change
    B. Helping the client compose a plan for change
    C. Allowing the client to establish a reasonable time period for change
    D. Writing up a behavioral plan and then asking the client to adhere to it

17. The open systems model of nursing care is driven by the principle that communication should be used by the nurse to 17.____

    A. promote wellness
    B. heal the client
    C. widen the client's support network
    D. help the client adapt to his or her environment

18. The most appropriate demonstration of critical thinking by an inexperienced nurse would occur when he 18.____

    A. asks the client many focused questions
    B. relies on what he has witnessed other nurses do in similar situations
    C. admits uncertainty about how to perform a procedure, and asking for help
    D. studies the institutional policies and procedures manual

19. A client is to undergo a test for occult blood in the stool. For three days prior to the test, it is important for the client to take each of the following precautions, EXCEPT to

    A. avoid oral iron supplements
    B. avoid alcohol or caffeine
    C. undergo an assessment for hemorrhoids
    D. avoid the ingestion of red meat

20. Which of the following processes in nursing diagnosis occurs FIRST?

    A. Making a decision on the problem based on validation
    B. Observing/noting changes in physical status
    C. Taking necessary steps to rule out other hypotheses
    D. Determining the possible alternatives that could have caused changes in physical status

21. A client will most likely respond favorably to a nurse's verbal communication if the nurse

    A. remains professional and uses medical and technical terms for conditions and procedures
    B. opens up and reveals something about himself during communication
    C. maintains the same tone of voice throughout the conversation
    D. uses consistency in both verbal and nonverbal communication

22. Serum osmolality values are used during the assessment of a client's fluid and electrolyte balance, primarily to measure the extent of

    A. hypervolemia
    B. fluid volume excess
    C. dehydration
    D. fluid volume deficit

23. Before reminding a client of the importance of consistently taking his prescribed medication on schedule, a nurse decides what tone of voice to use and what gestures, if any, will be used to reinforce the message. The nurse is engaging in a process known as

    A. verbal cues
    B. inductive bias
    C. sending
    D. encoding

24. "To Err is Human: Building a Safer Health System," the influential report published by the Institute of Medicine in 2000, between 44,000 and 98,000 people die in the United States each year from _____ more than die from motor vehicle accidents, breast cancer, or Alzheimer's disease.

    A. heart disease
    B. illegal drug use
    C. AIDS
    D. medical errors

25. A nurse is administering oxygen to a client with emphysema. The nurse uses an oxygen analyzer to monitor levels of oxygen, knowing that high levels of oxygen over long periods of time are most likely to cause   25.____

    A. hyperventilation
    B. damage to the retina and cornea
    C. irreversible brain damage
    D. pulmonary edema

KEY (CORRECT ANSWERS)

1.	C	11.	D
2.	B	12.	A
3.	C	13.	B
4.	C	14.	B
5.	C	15.	C
6.	C	16.	D
7.	A	17.	D
8.	B	18.	C
9.	B	19.	B
10.	B	20.	B

21. D
22. C
23. D
24. D
25. B

EXAMINATION SECTION
TEST 1

DIRECTIONS: Each question or incomplete statement is followed by several suggested answers or completions. Select the one that BEST answers the question or completes the statement. *PRINT THE LETTER OF THE CORRECT ANSWER IN THE SPACE AT THE RIGHT.*

1. The nurse-client relationship is characterized by each of the following, EXCEPT

   A. positive regard
   B. therapeutic self-disclosure
   C. abstraction
   D. empathy

2. Which of the following is an example of an open-ended question?

   A. Did you leave the bed to urinate last night?
   B. When did you first begin to notice the pain?
   C. Is somebody coming to pick you up this morning?
   D. What happened to your shoulder?

3. Of the following, which is LEAST likely to cause REM sleep deprivation?

   A. A regularly scheduled 60-hour work week
   B. Sleep apnea
   C. Barbiturates
   D. Alcohol

4. When assessing a client's communication abilities, a nurse needs to evaluate both the client's communication style and

   A. impairments or barriers to communication
   B. education level
   C. medical history
   D. posture

5. The term "aphagia" refers to

   A. the inability to swallow
   B. the inability to speak
   C. difficult or painful swallowing
   D. an absence of white blood cells

6. During the assessment phase, a nurse acquires each of the following items of data. Which would require validation?

   A. The client says she feels feverish
   B. The client's pulse is 102
   C. The client's blood pressure is 112/65
   D. The client's chart indicates a history of asthma

7. During the assessment interview, a nurse attempts to use active listening skills. Which of the following is an element of this skill set?

   A. Responding quickly to the client and trying to summarize the client's statements
   B. Interrupting the client only when clarification is needed
   C. Asking for crucial items of information
   D. Listening for principal themes in the client's communication

8. Each of the following is a recognized stage in the body's inflammatory response to infection, EXCEPT

   A. exudate
   B. vascular response
   C. passive immunity
   D. reparation

9. Generally, a humidifying device will be required when oxygen is administered to a client at a flow rate of _____ liters/minute or more.

   A. 2
   B. 4
   C. 6
   D. 8

10. During an assessment interview, a nurse attempts to assess the client's personal identity. Which of the following questions is an appropriate means of assessing this?

    A. What kind of people do you most enjoy being around?
    B. Do you have any meaningful relationships with family members?
    C. Do you think this problem has anything to do with your choices or behaviors?
    D. If you could change anything about yourself, what would it be?

11. Possible causes of polyuria include each of the following, EXCEPT

    A. extremely low fluid intake
    B. congestive heart failure
    C. intestinal obstruction
    D. liver failure

12. In nursing, a process recording is primarily useful for

    A. insuring that all interventions and medications are having the desired effects
    B. ensuring that the nurse adheres to an established care plan
    C. analyzing the effectiveness of nurse-client communication in modifying client behaviors
    D. establishing a therapeutic relationship

13. When a client develops contracts the human immunodeficiency virus (HIV), he loses _____ immunity.

    A. passive
    B. adaptive
    C. cellular
    D. humoral

14. A client with non-Hodgkin's lymphoma is receiving leurocristine. The nurse should make sure the client's diet is

   A. low-fat
   B. high in fluids but low in residue
   C. low in protein, but with increased iron
   D. high in fluids and dietary fiber

15. A client's medication order reads "Chlorpropamide 250 mg qd. The medication is available as Diabinese, .25 gram tablets. How many tablets should the nurse give to the client in one dose?

   A. half
   B. 1
   C. one-and-half
   D. 2

16. A sleep history taken during a nursing assessment typically includes each of the following, EXCEPT

   A. content of dreams
   B. bedtime rituals
   C. use of sleep medications
   D. client satisfaction with sleep

17. A 38-year-old client is admitted to the hospital with a diagnosis of chronic renal insufficiency. He is weak, hypotensive, and has low sodium and high potassium levels. The focus of his nursing care plan should be

   A. restoring electrolyte balance
   B. increasing urinary output
   C. increasing carbohydrate intake
   D. postural drainage

18. A client visits a clinic with a twisted ankle that has swollen. Of the following chronic conditions, which would contraindicate the use of ice on the ankle?

   A. Chronic obstructive pulmonary disease
   B. Osteoporosis
   C. Glaucoma
   D. Diabetes mellitus

19. Prior to a surgical procedure, a client asks the nurse to stay and pray with him and his wife. The nurse is an agnostic who does not attend church services and has never prayed before. The most appropriate nursing action would for the nurse to

   A. stay with the client and either join in the prayer or remain silent
   B. explain that prayer is not a part of her personal belief system
   C. try to explain with humor that she is an agnostic and her prayers are unlikely to do any good
   D. offer to have the hospital chaplain perform a service

20. Which of the following nursing interventions is LEAST appropriate for a client with chronic renal failure?

    A. Hourly assessment for hyper- or hypovolemia
    B. Promote maintenance of skin integrity
    C. Hourly assessment for signs of uremia
    D. Monitor and prevent changes in fluid and electrolyte balance

21. During auscultation, the nurse notes a high-pitched musical sound during expiration. This would be documented as

    A. rhonchi
    B. rales
    C. crepitations
    D. wheeze

22. Each of the following is involved in a typical nutritional assessment, EXCEPT

    A. the dietary history
    B. a comparison of weight to body build
    C. mid-upper arm circumference measurement
    D. girth measurements

23. Which of the following nursing diagnoses is written in PES format?

    A. Potential for impaired skin integrity related to immobility
    B. Impaired communication related to laryngectomy, as manifested by an inability to talk,
    C. At risk for aspiration
    D. Decreased caloric intake related to altered nutrition: Less than body requirements

24. A nurse is administering oxygen to a client with emphysema. An oxygen analyzer is used to monitor levels of oxygen, and is calibrated using room air, which is about _____ percent oxygen

    A. 10
    B. 20
    C. 40
    D. 60

25. A father is frustrated because his five-year-old son cannot stay dry at night. The most appropriate suggestion by the nurse would be that

    A. bedwetting is often a sign of an underlying psychological problem
    B. the father should ask the doctor about the possibility of prescribing Desmopressin
    C. while frustrating, bedwetting is a condition that is not normally appropriate for treatment until a child reaches the age of six or seven
    D. the child should be awakened at the same time every night to void his bladder

KEY (CORRECT ANSWERS)

1.	C		11.	A
2.	D		12.	C
3.	A		13.	C
4.	A		14.	D
5.	A		15.	B
6.	A		16.	A
7.	D		17.	A
8.	C		18.	D
9.	A		19.	A
10.	D		20.	A

21. D
22. D
23. B
24. B
25. C

TEST 2

DIRECTIONS: Each question or incomplete statement is followed by several suggested answers or completions. Select the one that BEST answers the question or completes the statement. *PRINT THE LETTER OF THE CORRECT ANSWER IN THE SPACE AT THE RIGHT.*

1. In planning a menu for a vegetarian client, the nurse will need to take special care that the client's food contains adequate amounts of

   A. protein
   B. carbohydrate
   C. fiber
   D. vitamin A

2. The word "macule" refers to a

   A. flat area of discoloration on the skin
   B. raised or elevated area
   C. blister-like raised area filled with fluid
   D. raised area containing pus

3. Which of the following is MOST likely to be the causative factor in ischemia?

   A. aneurysm
   B. respiratory distress
   C. atherosclerosis
   D. anemia

4. During the assessment phase of the nursing process, the nurse applies critical thinking when she

   A. thinks ahead to the therapeutic goals that are likely to be established
   B. asks closed-ended questions
   C. expresses doubt about the data provided by the client
   D. asks questions that are culturally sensitive

5. The most common infecting organism associated with nosocomial infections is

   A. Enterococcus
   B. Staphylococcus aureus
   C. Lactobacillus
   D. E. coli

6. In the following nursing diagnosis-Ineffective airway clearance related to decreased energy as manifested by an ineffective cough-the etiology of the diagnosis is represented by

   A. decreased energy
   B. an ineffective cough
   C. as manifested by
   D. ineffective airway clearance

7. A client with gastroenteritis and severe diarrhea is MOST at risk for losing excessive amounts of

   A. chloride
   B. potassium
   C. sodium
   D. phosphate

8. Which of the following behaviors-on the part of the nurse-is known to inhibit effective nurse-client communication?

   A. Maintaining silence
   B. Stating observations
   C. Paraphrasing
   D. Showing approval or disapproval

9. Typically, a nurse may facilitate pulmonary ventilation through each of the following means, EXCEPT

   A. suctioning
   B. stress reduction
   C. percussion
   D. hydration

10. Of the following, which as at greatest risk for developing an upper respiratory infection?

    A. 30-year-old with Stage I HIV infection
    B. 45-year-old pregnant client
    C. 60-year-old nonsmoker
    D. 4-year-old preschooler

11. While bathing a client, the nurse assesses the client's skin. Which of the following would necessitate a referral to another health professional?

    A. Pitted edema at the ankles
    B. Rough, flaking skin in exposed areas
    C. Keratosis pilaris
    D. Angular stomatitis

12. A client with hyperpnea

    A. is hyperventilating
    B. will need to exercise or otherwise raise his heart rate to improve blood oxygenation
    C. is experiencing an excessively high rate of alveolar ventilation
    D. presents a prolonged gasping inspiration followed by a very short, usually inefficient, expiration

13. A client with obesity is at greater risk of suffering _____ postoperatively than a client who is not obese.

    A. infection
    B. respiratory distress
    C. anaphylaxis
    D. delayed healing

14. A client has not adhered to a diet designed to manage her diabetes. Of the following, which statement or question by the nurse would be MOST likely to motivate the client to comply with dietary restrictions?

    A. I understand the diet is hard for you to stick to. Can you tell me why you find it so difficult?
    B. I'm having trouble understanding why you won't stick to the diet when we agreed upon it together.
    C. The diet has been designed to lengthen your life expectancy. Do you understand the consequences if you don't adhere to it?
    D. Is there somebody at home who can make sure you adhere to the diet?

15. Which of the following is an interdependent nursing action?

    A. Developing a nursing care plan
    B. Preparing a client for diagnostic tests
    C. Changing sterile dressings
    D. Teaching a client about hygiene

16. Which of the following communication tasks is typically part of the planning phase of the nursing process?

    A. Seeking the involvement of additional health resources
    B. Discussing methods of implementation with client
    C. Meeting the client
    D. Examining the need for adjustments and changes

17. For a client with mild hypothermia, the most appropriate intervention is

    A. administering warm IV fluids
    B. applying blankets
    C. applying an electric blanket
    D. turning up the room thermostat

18. Which of the following is NOT a therapeutic communication technique?

    A. Stating observations
    B. Clarifying
    C. Summarizing
    D. Offering opinions

19. During the psychosocial assessment of an 8-year-old client, it would be most helpful for the nurse to

    A. read the client a story or play a video prior to the interview
    B. provide some toys for the client to play with during the interview
    C. provide a nutritious snack
    D. establish a quiet and private setting

20. A nurse who wants a client to obtain maximum benefits after postural drainage should encourage the client to

    A. use bronchodilators
    B. remain lying down

C. elevate the feet
D. cough deeply

21. A nurse is developing a nutrition program for 6- and 7-year-old children. Given known health problems for children in this age group, the program should include

   A. distinguishing between HDL and LDL cholesterol
   B. identifying foods that contain water-soluble vitamins
   C. recognizing the importance of taking daily vitamin supplements
   D. identifying foods that may contribute to obesity

22. The most likely reaction of a client who has been recently transferred to the intensive care unit would be

   A. defiance
   B. confusion
   C. fear
   D. relief

23. When assessing a client's pain, the most important factor to consider is the

   A. likelihood that the pain will interfere with normal functioning
   B. client's own perception of the pain
   C. client's vital signs
   D. underlying cause of the pain

24. During the orientation stage of an initial interview with the client, the nurse should

   A. establish his authority and background in interviewing clients
   B. indicate what client health behaviors will be most desirable
   C. stick to closed questioning
   D. explain the purpose of the interview

25. A doctor has prescribed 5 tablespoons of an anti-diarrhea medication. The nurse's equipment is only marked for metric measurements. How many ml will the nurse administer?

   A. 12
   B. 32.5
   C. 75
   D. 130

KEY (CORRECT ANSWERS)

1.	A		11.	A
2.	A		12.	C
3.	C		13.	D
4.	D		14.	A
5.	D		15.	A
6.	A		16.	B
7.	B		17.	B
8.	D		18.	D
9.	B		19.	D
10.	D		20.	D

21.	D
22.	C
23.	B
24.	D
25.	C

TEST 3

DIRECTIONS: Each question or incomplete statement is followed by several suggested answers or completions. Select the one that BEST answers the question or completes the statement. *PRINT THE LETTER OF THE CORRECT ANSWER IN THE SPACE AT THE RIGHT.*

1. Nontherapeutic responses to client concerns include   1.____

    A. Reflecting
    B. Focusing
    C. Summarizing
    D. Probing

2. A nurse is working with a client who needs to learn how to perform her own colostomy   2.____
   care. It is most important that the nurse assess and facilitate

    A. readiness
    B. comfort
    C. motivation
    D. knowledge

3. The early treatment of diabetic acidosis would involve   3.____

    A. NPH insulin
    B. Respiratory intubation
    C. IV fluids
    D. Restricted sodium intake

4. Which of the following nursing skills is MOST likely to be required during the termination 4.____
   phase of the nurse-client relationship?

    A. Summarizing
    B. Clarifying
    C. Goal-setting
    D. Risk-taking

5. For a client who has a significant body odor, the most appropriate solution is   5.____

    A. a lesson in personal hygiene
    B. a bath or shower
    C. an alcohol-based deodorant
    D. antiperspirant

6. Symptoms of alveolar hyperventilation include   6.____

    A. numbness
    B. warm, dry skin
    C. pallor
    D. convulsions

7. The nurse is preparing to communicate discharge information to an elderly client of Chinese descent who speaks English well, but it is his second language. The best way to communicate with this client is to

   A. provide brief, simple explanations, and speak slowly
   B. provide some literature that he can read on his own later
   C. find an interpreter or family member to help
   D. provide comprehensive explanations of all information

8. Which phase of the nursing process involves the systematic and continuous collection, organization, validation, and documentation of data?

   A. Evaluating
   B. Assessing
   C. Planning
   D. Diagnosing

9. During the nursing assessment of a client with heart disease, the nurse becomes concerned that the client might be suffering from hypoxia. Each of the following is a clinical sign of hypoxia, EXCEPT

   A. intercostal retraction
   B. deep, rapid breaths
   C. cyanosis
   D. flaring nostrils

10. Digitalis preparations often involve the depletion of _____ as a side effect.

    A. phosphate
    B. potassium
    C. iron
    D. calcium

11. The label on a bottle of atropine states that the strength of each tablet is "gr 1/120." The client's medication order says that she should receive 0.5 g of atropine. The nurse should give the client _____ tablet.

    A. half
    B. 1
    C. one-and-half
    D. 2

12. A client complains of polyuria, pain on urination, and an unpleasant smell. The nurse calls for a urine sample. Which of the following is the most likely problem?

    A. Renal calculi
    B. Urinary tract infection
    C. Glomerulonephritis
    D. Acute renal failure

13. _____ infections are defined as those due to any aspect of medical therapy.

    A. Occult
    B. Nosocomial

C. Iatrogenic
D. Exanthematic

14. When ending an interview, the most appropriate communication technique for the nurse to use is usually

    A. a firm handshake
    B. reflecting
    C. summarizing
    D. self-disclosure

15. A 13-year-old client is experiencing painful abdominal cramps during menstruation. The most appropriate intervention for this would be to instruct the client to

    A. perform mild stretching exercises of the lower back and abdominal muscles
    B. rest and apply an ice pack to the abdomen
    C. decrease fluid intake
    D. rest and apply warmth to the abdomen

16. A nurse is developing an initial plan of care for a client. The plan should include

    A. a request for possible psychological consultation
    B. the client's vital signs on admission
    C. a nursing diagnosis
    D. a list of medications currently taken by the client

17. A client is about to undergo an adrenalectomy. It is MOST important for the nurse to insure _____ during the preoperative period.

    A. adequate nutrition
    B. increased fluid intake
    C. complete rest
    D. electrolyte balance

18. Which of the following clients might be legally allowed to give informed consent to a medical procedure?

    A. A client who is under sedation
    B. A client who experiences intermittent episodes of dementia who appears lucid at the time of consent
    C. An unconscious client
    D. A client whose injury or disability does not enable her to sign the consent form

19. A client who has recently suffered a laceration to her forehead complains of a throbbing localized pain on the surface of her head. This type of pain is best described as

    A. somatic
    B. neuropathic
    C. cutaneous
    D. visceral

20. A nursing care plan includes the goal of appropriate client response to stimuli. Which of the following outcomes would MOST clearly show that this goal has been met?

    A. Client is able to formulate sounds within 24 hours of admission
    B. Client and family openly discuss plans for discharge with a social worker by the fifth day of hospitalization
    C. Client is able to transmit a clear message to a nurse or family member by the second day of hospitalization
    D. Client is able to nonverbally acknowledge the receipt of a verbal message within 24 hours of admission

21. To examine the size of a client's liver, the nurse moves her hands over the surface of the client's abdomen. This examination technique is known as

    A. auscultation
    B. percussion
    C. palpation
    D. inspection

22. In communicating with toddlers or preschoolers, a nurse should be sure to

    A. prevent the child from handling equipment
    B. avoid nonverbal cues
    C. deflect difficult questions by offering a toy or snack
    D. focus the conversation on the child's personal needs and concerns

23. Which of the following is an example of ablative surgery?

    A. Mitral valve replacement
    B. Colostomy
    C. Tonsillectomy
    D. Arthroplasty

24. Likely causes of fluid volume deficit include each of the following, EXCEPT

    A. excess steroid intake
    B. bleeding
    C. third-space movement
    D. decreased fluid intake

25. A client has been placed on a low-residue diet. Which of the following foods would NOT be allowed?

    A. Oatmeal
    B. Butter
    C. Cottage Cheese
    D. Canned, peeled vegetables

KEY (CORRECT ANSWERS)

1.	D		11.	B
2.	A		12.	B
3.	C		13.	C
4.	A		14.	C
5.	B		15.	D
6.	A		16.	C
7.	A		17.	C
8.	B		18.	D
9.	B		19.	C
10.	B		20.	D

21. C
22. D
23. C
24. A
25. A

EXAMINATION SECTION
TEST 1

DIRECTIONS: Each question or incomplete statement is followed by several suggested answers or completions. Select the one that BEST answers the question or completes the statement. *PRINT THE LETTER OF THE CORRECT ANSWER IN THE SPACE AT THE RIGHT.*

1. Normal inspiration is an active process that uses the diaphragm and external intercostal muscles.
   Ineffective breathing patterns can be manifested by all of the following EXCEPT

   A. use of accessory muscles for respiration
   B. increased breath sounds in lung segments
   C. paradoxical respiratory movement
   D. restlessness, anxiety, and diaphoresis

   1.____

2. Postural drainage is indicated for patients who have difficulty clearing secretions due to airway obstruction and/or excessive mucus production.
   Signs of airway obstruction include

   A. tachycardia
   B. increased breath sounds with no crackles or gurgles
   C. increased oxygen saturation
   D. decreased respiratory rate

   2.____

3. Therapeutic percussion is typically provided while the patient is in various PD positions.
   Percussions and vibrations are CONTRAINDICATED in

   A. spinal anesthesia
   C. subcutaneous emphysema
   B. thoracic skin grafts
   D. all of the above

   3.____

4. It may be inappropriate to simply administer oxygen without conducting a thorough patient assessment to determine the cause of the hypoxemic event.
   Oxygen therapy is commonly prescribed in the initial treatment of all of the following conditions EXCEPT

   A. acute myocardial infarction
   B. tuberculosis
   C. severe trauma
   D. immediately following surgery or extubation

   4.____

5. Breathing oxygen concentrations greater than 50% for more than 24 hours can cause injury to the lung tissue or oxygen toxicity.
   Early signs of oxygen toxicity include
   I. dyspnea, cough, lethargy, and vomiting
   II. restlessness
   III. retrosternal chest pain
   IV. hemoptasis
   The CORRECT answer is:

   A. I, II, III
   C. I, III, IV
   B. I, II, IV
   D. II, IV

   5.____

49

6. Some patients continue oxygen therapy following discharge. Indications for home oxygen therapy include all of the following EXCEPT

   A. pulmonary hypertension
   B. recurring congestive heart failure
   C. anemia
   D. sleep apnea syndrome

7. Oxygen will not explode, but will cause something on fire to burn much faster. Important precautionary measures to prevent fire include

   A. no smoking in any room where oxygen is being used
   B. keep equipment at least 10 feet away from any open flame
   C. do not use oily lotions, face creams, grease, or lip balms around oxygen equipment
   D. all of the above

8. A transtracheal oxygen catheter is a thin, teflon-coated tube that is surgically placed into the trachea.
   Complications of transtracheal oxygen therapy include all of the following EXCEPT

   A. inflammation   B. thin secretions
   C. bleeding   D. infection

9. A metered-dose inhaler is a pressurized canister which releases an aerosol containing the drug suspended in a fluorocarbon gas stream.
   The nurse should provide the patient with instructions to

   A. assemble the inhaler
   B. shake the inhaler to mix the medication and propellent
   C. remove the cap from the mouthpiece
   D. all of the above

10. Artificial airways are devices designed to maintain patent communication between the tracheobronchial tree and the air supply in the external environment.
    Indications for an endotracheal tube include all of the following EXCEPT

    A. temporary measures for airway obstruction
    B. mechanical ventilation
    C. protection of nasal mucosa
    D. management of secretions

11. The main indication for the insertion of a nasal airway is to protect the nasal mucosa from the trauma of frequent passage of suction catheters.
    A MAJOR disadvantage of nasal airway insertion is

    A. it does not prevent occlusion of upper airway by tongue
    B. potential inability to speak
    C. potential for aspiration
    D. potential for laryngeal damage

12. For long-term use, tracheostomy is preferred over endotracheal intubation. Advantages of tracheostomy tubes include all of the following EXCEPT

    A. direct communication with trachea
    B. longer tube length results in less airway resistance than with endotracheal tubes
    C. easily tolerated by patients
    D. avoidance of trauma to larynx

13. Complications of intubation can be mechanical or physiologic in nature. _____ is a physiologic, not a mechanical, complication.

    A. Tube displacement
    B. Obstruction
    C. Aspiration
    D. Loss of cuff seal

14. Nursing diagnoses for patients on mechanical ventilation include nursing diagnoses common to intubated patients, such as

    A. inadequate gas exchange related to increased secretions, interstitial edema, and shunt
    B. high risk for decreased cardiac output related to decreased venous return
    C. anxiety related to mechanical ventilation and severity of illness
    D. all of the above

15. Acute sinusitis commonly accompanies or follows an upper respiratory tract infection. Of the following, the LEAST commonly involved organism is

    A. C. defficle
    B. H. influenzae
    C. S. pyogens
    D. S. pneumoniae

16. Anaerobic pathogens are the most common infectious cause of chronic sinusitis. Non-infectious contributors to chronic sinusitis include all of the following EXCEPT

    A. smoking
    B. amphetamine abuse
    C. habitual nasal sprays or inhalants
    D. history of allergy

17. Rhinitis is commonly caused by viral infection, as in acute rhinitis, or the common cold, coryza.
    Known organisms in acute viral rhinitis include
    I. rhinovirus
    II. influenza and para-influenza
    III. infectious mononucleosis
    IV. coxsackie virus
    The CORRECT answer is:

    A. I, II, III
    B. II, III
    C. I, II, IV
    D. I, II, III, IV

18. Nursing interventions to educate patients with rhinitis in order to prevent further infection include all of the following EXCEPT

    A. disposing of tissues properly
    B. using cloth handkerchiefs
    C. using good handwashing techniques
    D. covering mouth and nose when coughing and sneezing

19. Nasal obstruction is commonly caused by displacement of the nasal septum from the midline position.
Common results of nasal deviation include

    A. nasal obstruction
    B. postnasal drip
    C. epistaxis
    D. all of the above

20. The priority of goals established for the patient with epistaxis will depend on the severity of the problem and the presence or absence of associated complications. APPROPRIATE goals for patients with epistaxis include

    A. normal vital signs and level of consciousness
    B. adequate caloric intake
    C. pain relief
    D. all of the above

21. Nursing interventions while taking care of a patient with epistaxis include all of the following EXCEPT

    A. immediate assessment of vital signs
    B. positioning of the patient with foot end of the bed elevated
    C. pressure applied to the nose
    D. coaching in mouth breathing

22. When evaluating the care of a patient with epistaxis, the nurse considers which of the following assessment parameters?
    I. Respiratory accessory muscles should not be used.
    II. Cyanosis and diaphoresis should be absent.
    III. Mucus membrane should remain pink and moist.
    The CORRECT answer is:

    A. I only   B. I, II   C. I, II, III   D. II, III

23. The priority of goals established for the patient with a nasal fracture will depend on the severity of the problem and the presence or absence of associated complications. Appropriate goals for a patient with this problem include all of the following EXCEPT

    A. patent airway and normal blood gas levels
    B. elevated body temperature
    C. pain relief
    D. verbalization of acceptance of temporary disfigurement

24. The most common form of laryngeal cancer is squamous cell carcinoma.
The one of the following which is NOT a risk factor for laryngeal squamous cell carcinoma is

    A. cocaine abuse
    B. prolonged use of tobacco and alcohol
    C. exposure to radiation
    D. voice abuse

25. The earliest symptom of laryngeal cancer is hoarseness, or voice change.
Later manifestations include all of the following EXCEPT

    A. increasing dyspnea
    B. hematemesis
    C. dysphagia
    D. hemoptysis

KEY (CORRECT ANSWERS)

1. B
2. A
3. D
4. B
5. A

6. C
7. D
8. B
9. D
10. C

11. A
12. B
13. C
14. D
15. A

16. B
17. C
18. B
19. D
20. D

21. B
22. C
23. B
24. A
25. B

TEST 2

DIRECTIONS: Each question or incomplete statement is followed by several suggested answers or completions. Select the one that BEST answers the question or completes the statement. *PRINT THE LETTER OF THE CORRECT ANSWER IN THE SPACE AT THE RIGHT.*

1. An important role of the nurse is to instruct and assist the patient in producing an effective cough.
   Factors that influence the ability to cough include all of the following EXCEPT

   A. analgesia may be needed before cough exercise
   B. oral hydration using ice chips or sips of water can make coughing easier
   C. a lying down position is the most effective and comfortable position
   D. splinting a painful area during coughing with gentle hand pressure helps the patient cough

   1.____

2. Chronic obstructive pulmonary disease (COPD) is a broad term used to describe conditions characterized by chronic obstruction to expiratory air flow.
   Complications of COPD include all of the following EXCEPT

   A. acute respiratory failure
   B. tuberculosis
   C. cor pulmonale
   D. pneumothorax

   2.____

3. The priority goals of nursing intervention for patients with acute exacerbation of COPD are the maintenance of adequate oxygenation, ventilation, and airway clearance. The patient should display

   A. clear breath sounds with no crackles
   B. respiratory rate between 12-20 breaths/minute at rest
   C. arterial PO_2 at patient's normal baseline
   D. all of the above

   3.____

4. The etiological factors of asthma are not completely understood, but it is clear that asthma can develop after exposure to a variety of substances.
   Asthma is characterized by all of the following EXCEPT

   A. hemoptosis
   B. reversible airway obstruction
   C. airway inflammation
   D. airway hyperresponsiveness

   4.____

5. The severity of an asthma attack is reflected by the degree of airflow obstruction, level of oxygenation, and nature of breathing patterns.
   Patients at increased risk for life-threatening asthma attacks do NOT include those

   A. less than 1 year old
   B. with PEFR or FEV_1 below 25% of predicted level
   C. with PCO_2 below 40 mmHg
   D. with wide daily fluctuation in PEFR or FEV_1

   5.____

6. Which of the following is associated with an acute asthma attack?
   I. Impaired gas exchange related to ventilation-per-fusion mismatch, impaired diffusion, or arterio-venous shunting
   II. Fatigue related to increased efforts to breathe
   III. Fluid volume deficit related to increased intake and decreased insensible loss

   The CORRECT answer is:

   A. I only
   B. I, II
   C. I, II, III
   D. II, III

7. Outcome criteria for a patient with asthma include all of the following EXCEPT that the patient

   A. maintain $PaCO_2$ at approximately 40 mmHg
   B. have clear breath sounds on auscultation
   C. maintain PaO_2 at approximately 50 mmHg
   D. report no breathlessness at rest and minimal with activities

8. Restrictive lung diseases encompass a vast array of disorders that lead to decreased lung inflation.
   A hallmark of all restrictive disorders, regardless of cause, is

   A. decreased lung volume
   B. decreased breath sounds
   C. decreased vital capacity
   D. increased residual volume

9. Restrictive disorders are associated with

   A. ineffective breathing pattern related to increased lung inflation
   B. impaired gas exchange related to increased surface area for diffusion
   C. activity intolerance related to impaired gas exchange
   D. all of the above

10. Adult respiratory distress syndrome (ARDS) is a common problem, and 65% of cases are fatal.
    Major causes of ARDS include all of the following EXCEPT

    A. multiple sclerosis
    B. multiple blood transfusions
    C. aspiration of gastric contents
    D. trauma and sepsis

11. It has been reported that inspiratory pressures greater than 70 cm H_2O are associated with a 43% risk of barotrauma.
    Risk factors for barotrauma include

    A. low residual volume
    B. large tidal volume
    C. low levels of PEEP
    D. low peak airway pressure

12. Barotrauma is the presence of air outside the alveolus and is manifested by
    I. pulmonary interstitial emphysema
    II. pneumomediastinum
    III. tension lung cysts
    The CORRECT answer is:

    A. I, II
    B. II only
    C. I, III
    D. I, II, III

13. The aim of therapy in a patient of ARDS is to support lung function until healing occurs and to prevent the development of complications related to medical therapy and the underlying disease process.
    Goals of therapeutic management include

    A. optimizing gas exchange
    B. maintaining adequate tissue perfusion
    C. controlling the underlying problem that precipitated ARDS
    D. all of the above

14. Nursing care for the patient with ARDS is planned to maintain respiratory and hemodynamic stability.
    Outcome criteria for the patient include all of the following EXCEPT

    A. PaO_2 below 60 mmHg on 40% FIO_2 with a shunt fraction of less than 20%
    B. peak airway pressure below 40-50 mmHg
    C. skin remains intact
    D. stable weight

15. Generally, mechanical ventilation of COPD patients is avoided if at all possible. Mechanical ventilation is NOT deemed necessary when

    A. conservative therapy has failed to improve hypoxemia/acidosis or has resulted in progressive somnolence
    B. the patient is exhausted
    C. the patient has severe hyperoxemia and alkalosis and is unable to cooperate because of altered mental status
    D. the patient is unable to expectorate secretions

16. The nursing care for COPD patients in acute respiratory failure is planned to achieve which of the following outcomes?

    A. Breathing pattern and arterial blood gas levels return to prefailure levels
    B. Lungs clear to auscultation
    C. Airway remains patent
    D. All of the above

17. Pneumonia is an inflammation of the lower respiratory tract that involves the lung parenchyma, including alveoli and supportive structures.
    The organism MOST commonly involved in the causation of community acquired pneumonia is

    A. klebsiella pneumonia
    B. staphylococcus aureus
    C. streptococcus pnemoniae
    D. pseudomonas aeruginosa

18. Hospital acquired, or nosocomial, pneumonias are LEAST commonly caused by

    A. pseudomonas aeruginosa
    B. klebsiella pneumonia
    C. streptococcus pneumoniae
    D. staphylococcus aureus

19. Which of the following persons are at INCREASED risk for aspiration pneumonia?
    I. Drug abusers
    II. Impaired gag or swallowing reflex
    III. Alcoholics
    The CORRECT answer is:

    A. I, II
    B. I, II, III
    C. I, III
    D. II only

20. Viral pneumonia in immunosuppressed patients is MOST commonly caused by

    A. cytomegalovirus
    B. influenza virus type A
    C. para influenza virus
    D. respiratory syncitial virus

21. Priorities for planning nursing care of patients with pneumonia include treatment of the infection, maintenance of adequate oxygenation, and maintenance of patent airways. While observing for evidence of complications, such as respiratory failure, appropriate outcome criteria include all of the following EXCEPT

    A. breath sounds clear with coughing
    B. PaO$_2$ less than 55 mmHg at rest and with activities
    C. sputum expectorated with minimal effort
    D. appetite returns to normal baseline

22. Tuberculosis can be highly contagious and is transmitted by airborne mechanisms from infected persons.
    The one of the following which is NOT a common cause of tuberculosis is

    A. mycobacterium tuberculosis
    B. M. bovis
    C. M. leprae
    D. M. africanum

23. Patients at INCREASED risk for drug-resistant tuberculosis include

    A. foreign-born persons from Asia, Africa, and Latin America
    B. persons with positive bacteriology after 3 months of therapy
    C. contacts of known or suspected drug-resistant cases
    D. all of the above

24. Lung cancer is a serious health problem in the United States.
    Risk factors for lung cancer include all of the following EXCEPT

    A. cigarette smoking
    B. amphetamine abuse
    C. asbestos exposure
    D. exposure to arsenic, radon, and chromium

25. Hematological manifestations associated with lung cancer include 25.____
   A. anemia
   B. disseminated intravascular coagulation
   C. thrombophlebitis
   D. all of the above

KEY (CORRECT ANSWERS)

1.	C		11.	B
2.	B		12.	D
3.	D		13.	D
4.	A		14.	A
5.	C		15.	C
6.	B		16.	D
7.	C		17.	C
8.	A		18.	C
9.	C		19.	B
10.	A		20.	A

21. B
22. C
23. D
24. B
25. D

EXAMINATION SECTION
TEST 1

DIRECTIONS: Each question or incomplete statement is followed by several suggested answers or completions. Select the one that BEST answers the question or completes the statement. *PRINT THE LETTER OF THE CORRECT ANSWER IN THE SPACE AT THE RIGHT.*

1. Radiation therapy is administered to selected patients with lung cancer. Toxic side effects of radiation therapy include   1.____

    A. esophagitis
    B. fibrosis
    C. pneumonitis
    D. all of the above

2. The priority for nursing care of patients with lung cancer is maintenance of adequate gas exchange and airway clearance while trying to keep patients as comfortable as possible. For a patient in the acute phase, outcome criteria might include all of the following EXCEPT   2.____

    A. PaO$_2$ is less than 55 mmHg at rest and with activities
    B. sputum is expectorated with minimal effort
    C. patient maintains realistic level of activity
    D. patient sleeps comfortably at night and feels rested in the morning

3. Nursing interventions for patients with dyspnea related to lung cancer should include   3.____

    A. relaxation techniques
    B. proper positioning and controlling the environment
    C. breathing techniques, such as pursed-lip breathing
    D. all of the above

4. When a patient is admitted to the emergency room with chest trauma, the primary goal of nursing care is to maintain a patent airway, adequate ventilation, and adequate circulation while assessing the extent of injury. Outcome criteria for this patient include   4.____

    A. arterial PO$_2$ is maintained below 55 mmHg
    B. patient sleeps appropriate number of hours and reports feeling rested
    C. breath sounds are unclear with adventitious sounds
    D. patient reports maximal respiratory discomfort

5. Atherosclerosis is the major pathologic process by which lipid deposits occur in the intimal and subintimal layers of the artery. *Controllable* risk factors for atherosclerosis include all of the following EXCEPT   5.____

    A. diabetes mellitus
    B. hyperlipidemia
    C. family history
    D. smoking

6. Smoking is the most consistent risk factor in the literature on peripheral vascular occlusive disease.
Of the following, only _____ is NOT among the effects of smoking on the cardiovascular system.   6.____

    A. increased systolic blood pressure
    B. vasodilatation

C. reduced exercise tolerance
D. increased heart rate

7. Effects of smoking on the blood include
   I. hemoconcentration
   II. decreased fibrinogen levels
   III. shorter platelet survival
   IV. decreased viscosity
   The CORRECT answer is:

   A. I, II
   B. I, III
   C. II, III, IV
   D. I, II, III, IV

8. The MOST common areas for developing atherosclerotic plaques include

   A. major arterial bifurcations
   B. aorta
   C. superficial femoral artery at Hunter's canal
   D. all of the above

9. Hyperlipidemia has been implicated in the development of arterial occlusive disease. Lipid effects as a result of smoking do NOT include increased

   A. total cholesterol
   B. HDL cholesterol
   C. permeability of vessels to lipids
   D. none of the above

10. Atherosclerosis is asymptomatic until a critical stenosis occurs in an artery. Effects of smoking on the blood vessels include all of the following EXCEPT

    A. decreased myointimal proliferation
    B. decreased oxygenation of vessel walls
    C. increased permeability of endothelium
    D. endothelial injury

11. Nursing management for the patient with atherosclerosis is planned so that the patient will

    A. adopt protective measures against injury of impaired tissue
    B. practice behavior to increase collateral circulation
    C. state the relationship between atherosclerosis and risk factors
    D. all of the above

12. Nursing interventions for patients with atherosclerosis are primarily for secondary and tertiary prevention.
    Patient education guidelines for antihyperlipidemic agents include all of the following EXCEPT

    A. mix medication with water or juice; do not take it dry
    B. take medication one hour before or 6 hours after other medications to avoid interference with absorption of other drugs
    C. do not take medications with meals
    D. report any gastrointestinal or other symptoms

13. An extranatomic bypass is a graft in the subcutaneous tissue instead of the abdominal cavity.
High risk patients who may benefit from extranatomic bypass include all of the following EXCEPT those   13._____

   A. with intraabdominal infection or infected graft
   B. under 60 years of age
   C. with aortoenteric fistula present
   D. with morbid obesity

14. In the post-operative nursing care of a patient with a femoral-to-popliteal or femoral-to-distal tibial bypass graft, it is NOT necessary to   14._____

   A. assess the wound for bleeding or swelling from hematoma formation
   B. avoid flexing the groin or knees more than 45 degrees for extended periods
   C. allow the patient to put powder, lotion, or other materials in the groin to keep it wet
   D. avoid compression or circumferential dressings

15. The one of the following which is NOT among the goals of nursing management of a patient with chronic arterial occlusive disease of the extremities is that the patient   15._____

   A. manage activity within his own limits
   B. have minimum tissue perfusion
   C. have decreased pain
   D. practice self-care to avoid tissue damage

16. The operative mortality rate for elective aneurysm repair is approximately 5%, as opposed to 50-80% for the ruptured aneurysm.
Post-operative nursing care of such a patient should include   16._____

   A. maintaining adequate fluid balance
   B. having adequate peripheral tissue perfusion
   C. having knowledge of discharge instructions
   D. all of the above

17. Raynaud's disease is the condition most often seen in patients with vasospastic disorders.
Nursing care of a patient with Raynaud's disease aims to achieve   17._____

   A. demonstration of knowledge of measures to prevent recurrent episodes
   B. skin temperature, color, and pulse within patient's normal limits
   C. decreased number of episodes of arterial spasm
   D. all of the above

18. Patient education and emotional support are important aspects of nursing care.
To avoid Raynaud's disease symptoms, patient education should include all of the following guidelines EXCEPT   18._____

   A. smoking cessation
   B. avoiding hot weather
   C. managing stress
   D. avoiding vibration

19. Thoracic outlet syndrome is a set of upper extremity symptoms resulting from neurovascular compression in the thoracic outlet area.
    These symptoms result from compression of the brachial nerve plexus and the subclavian artery and vein by all of the following structures EXCEPT the

    A. scalenus posterior muscles
    B. clavicle
    C. scalenus anterior muscles
    D. first rib

    19.____

20. A nurse is teaching a patient about thoracic outlet syndromes.
    It is TRUE concerning the nursing care of this patient that the

    A. overweight patient won't benefit from a weight reduction plan
    B. nurse can reinforce the exercise program and refer the patient to physical therapy
    C. nurse may also provide emotional and financial support to the patient
    D. all of the above

    20.____

21. In the past, medications have been the major mode of therapy for patients with hypertension. Greater emphasis is now being placed on nonpharmacologic approaches by the National Committee on Hypertension.
    These nonpharmacological approaches do NOT include

    A. sodium restriction
    C. weight control
    B. restricted water intake
    D. alcohol restriction

    21.____

22. Vasodilators used in the treatment of hypertension act by decreasing peripheral vascular resistance. Their side effects include all of the following EXCEPT

    A. headaches
    C. bronchospasm
    B. orthostatic hypotension
    D. fluid retention

    22.____

23. Six criteria have been established by the Joint National Committee on Detection, Evaluation, and Treatment of Hypertension to ensure accurate blood pressure measurement.
    Of the following, the INCORRECT statement is:

    A. Patient should be in a lying down position with arm positioned above heart level
    B. Measurement should begin after 5 minutes of quiet rest
    C. Appropriate cuff size must be used to ensure accurate measurement
    D. Both the systolic and diastolic blood pressures should be recorded

    23.____

24. The decision to begin anti-hypertensive therapy is usually a lifetime commitment for a patient. It is imperative that the nurse, as the patient's advocate and educator, answer the patient's questions thoroughly before the patient engages in therapy.
    Subjects for the nurse to evaluate include

    A. age: young people have higher renin levels than older ones
    B. weight: excessive weight tends to occur with increasing age
    C. level of blood pressure: mild hypertension may be treated nonpharmacologically
    D. all of the above

    24.____

25. Cardiopulmonary arrest in the hospital setting commonly results in a *Code* situation. In a code situation, someone from the team is usually REQUIRED to
     I. manage the airway and IV access
     II. perform chest compressions
     III. document all activities
   The CORRECT answer is:

   A. I, II
   B. II, III
   C. I, II, III
   D. III *only*

25.____

KEY (CORRECT ANSWERS)

1. D
2. A
3. D
4. B
5. C

6. B
7. B
8. D
9. B
10. A

11. D
12. C
13. B
14. C
15. B

16. D
17. D
18. B
19. A
20. B

21. B
22. C
23. A
24. D
25. C

TEST 2

DIRECTIONS: Each question or incomplete statement is followed by several suggested answers or completions. Select the one that BEST answers the question or completes the statement. *PRINT THE LETTER OF THE CORRECT ANSWER IN THE SPACE AT THE RIGHT.*

1. Approximately 50,000 to 60,000 people in the United States die each year from pulmonary emboli that originate from deep vein thrombosis (DVT).
Disease processes that predispose the patient to DVT include all of the following EXCEPT

    A. congenital heart failure
    B. tuberculosis
    C. sepsis
    D. myocardial infarction

    1.____

2. A nurse taking care of a patient with deep vein thrombosis should instruct the patient to

    A. take anticoagulant at a different time each day
    B. take aspirin or ibuprofen
    C. use soft brush and electric razor
    D. all of the above

    2.____

3. A nurse is assessing a patient for risk factors for deep vein thrombosis and pulmonary embolism.
Patient instruction should include all of the following advice EXCEPT:

    A. Do not sit or cross legs for prolonged periods
    B. If traveling, exercise at least every 12 hours
    C. Do not wear constrictive clothing
    D. Know the classic signs of pulmonary embolism

    3.____

4. Atrial tachycardia describes an ectopic supraventricular rhythm with a ventricular rate ranging from 140 to 250 beats per minute.
ECG criteria for diagnosis do NOT include

    A. P'-P' interval may be slightly irregular
    B. ectopic P waves look alike and closely resemble sinus P waves
    C. QRS is wide unless intraventricular conduction is disturbed
    D. P'R interval is short

    4.____

5. Atrioventricular blocks (AVBs) represent disturbed conduction of the electrical impulse between the atria and ventricles.
AVBs may be produced in association with all of the following EXCEPT

    A. reduced vagal tone
    B. myocardial ischemia
    C. electrolyte imbalances
    D. compression of conduction tissue

    5.____

6. A pacemaker is an electronic device that delivers a controlled electrical stimulus to the heart through electrodes that are placed in contact with heart muscles. Permanent pacing is indicated in cases of
    I. mild palpitations
    II. sick sinus syndrome
    III. myocardial necrosis
The CORRECT answer is:

A. I, II
B. I *only*
C. I, II, III
D. II, III

7. Congestive heart failure represents the inability of the heart to pump enough blood to meet tissue requirements for oxygen.
Primary pathologic conditions associated with acute and chronic forms of heart failure include

A. hypertension
B. valvular heart diseases
C. cardiomyopathies
D. all of the above

8. The signs and symptoms of heart failure reflect the status of intrinsic compensatory mechanisms and vary according to the degree of failure.
Physiologic, endocrine, and renal responses to heart failure include

A. decreased antidiuretic hormone
B. decreased glomerular filtration rate
C. decreased aldosterone
D. increased urinary output

9. Nursing advice for patients of coronary artery disease concerning the avoidance of activities that may increase myocardial oxygen demand include all of the following EXCEPT

A. avoid excessive caffeine intake
B. be sure to get enough physical activity after meals
C. avoid activities known to cause anginal pain, e.g., extremes of temperature, exertion, and attitudes
D. avoid alcohol

10. Myocardial infarction (MI) is an acute process in which myocardial tissues experience a severe and prolonged decrease in oxygen supply because of a disruption or deficiency in coronary blood flow, causing necrosis or *death* of the tissue.
Of the following, only _____ is NOT among the causes of MI.

A. acute coronary thrombosis
B. amphetamine abuse
C. coronary artery spasm
D. cocaine abuse

11. A patient of MI is discharged from the hospital.
Nursing advice for the progression of activities for this patient should include all of the following EXCEPT

A. increase activity level gradually
B. avoid lifting heavy objects, isometric activities, straining, or pushing

C. eat two or three large meals rather than several small meals per day
D. ensure adequate sleep with daily rest periods

12. In a case of myocardial infarction, activity progression is based on the patient's physiologic response.
Activity tolerance is determined using which of the following criteria?

    A. Heart rate increase less than 20 beats/minute
    B. No decrease in systolic blood pressure
    C. No chest pain, dyspnea, extreme fatigue, or dysrhythmias
    D. All of the above

13. When instructing a discharging patient of MI, the nurse should tell him to report IMMEDIATELY if he experiences

    A. increased shortness of breath
    B. rapid weight gain
    C. dizziness or fainting
    D. all of the above

14. Pericarditis refers to an inflammation of the pericardium, the membrane surrounding the heart. Autoimmune causes of pericarditis include all of the following EXCEPT

    A. tuberculosis
    B. Dressier's syndrome
    C. rheumatic disease
    D. systemic lupus erythematosus

15. Dilated cardiomyopathy is a disorder of the myocardium characterized by impaired contractility and pumping ability.
Its precipitating factors do NOT include

    A. immunologic disorders
    B. pregnancy
    C. uncontrolled hypotension
    D. chronic alcohol ingestion

16. Nursing goals for patients must be tailored to meet the needs of each individual, considering the type of cardiomyopathy and the age, social setting, and severity of illness of the patient. Goals for the patient aim to ensure that

    A. patient can tolerate mild activity and build activity into each day
    B. respirations are comfortable and breath sounds are clear
    C. anxiety is channeled constructively, with reduction in stress
    D. all of the above

17. When cardiac surgery is performed for coronary artery obstruction, a coronary artery bypass graft (CABG) is used.
All of the following complications may occur as a result of cardiac surgery or the use of a cardiopulmonary bypass machine EXCEPT

    A. hyperthermia   B. coagulation defects
    C. hemodilution   D. reduced lung compliance

18. Infective endocarditis is an infection of the endocardial layer of the heart. 18.____
Infecting bacterial causes include

    A. staphylococcus aureus   B. pseudomonas
    C. enterococcus   D. all of the above

19. Sickle cell anemia is a disorder of abnormal hemoglobin, also termed hemoglobinopathy, 19.____
in which one or both of the polypeptide chains are abnormal.
Management of pain episodes associated with sickle cell anemia include all of the following EXCEPT

    A. cold application to joints
    B. analgesics
    C. rest
    D. hydration

20. Chronic mitral regurgitation, also known as mitral insufficiency, is often seen with mitral 20.____
stenosis. Rheumatic heart disease is the predominant cause.
Other causes of mitral regurgitation include
    I. infective endocarditis
    II. mitral valve prolapse
    III. leakage through a prosthetic valve
The CORRECT answer is:

    A. I, II   B. II *only*
    C. I, II, III   D. II, III

21. Because such a large number of elderly people are affected by a vitamin B_{12} deficiency, 21.____
causing megaloblastic anemia, it is important to assess the elderly in this area. This is particularly important since this deficiency may not be diagnosed because older adults frequently attribute signs of deficiency to age and do not seek medical assistance. Signs and symptoms of vitamin B_{12} deficiency include all of the following EXCEPT

    A. sore and beefy tongue
    B. osteoarthritis
    C. paranoia
    D. numbness and tingling peripherally

22. Leukemia is a group of malignant diseases of the bone marrow and is characterized by 22.____
an unregulated proliferation of cells of hematopoietic origin.
Predisposing genetic abnormalities for leukemia include all of the following EXCEPT

    A. Down's syndrome
    B. fragile *X* syndrome
    C. Fanconi's anemia
    D. Wiskott-Aldrich's syndrome

23. Tumor lysis syndrome is a major complication of chemotherapy in acute lymphocytic leukemia. 23.____
The one of the following which is NOT a complication of tumor lysis syndrome is

    A. hypokalemia   B. hyperphosphatemia
    C. hypocalcemia   D. hyperuricemia

24. Multiple myeloma is a neoplastic proliferation of plasma cells, characterized by lytic bone lesions, anemia, and homogeneous serum or urinary globulin elevation. Nursing interventions in this case aims to do all of the following EXCEPT

   A. prevent infection
   B. keep patient immobile
   C. provide pain relief
   D. provide adequate hydration

25. Disseminated intravascular coagulation (DIC) is an acquired syndrome of clotting cascade overstimulation. Predisposing hematological causes of DIC do NOT include

   A. blood transfusion reaction
   B. sickle cell crisis
   C. iron deficiency anemia
   D. thalassemia major

KEY (CORRECT ANSWERS)

1. B
2. C
3. B
4. C
5. A
6. D
7. D
8. B
9. B
10. B

11. C
12. D
13. D
14. A
15. C
16. D
17. A
18. D
19. A
20. C

21. B
22. B
23. A
24. B
25. C

EXAMINATION SECTION
TEST 1

DIRECTIONS: Each question or incomplete statement is followed by several suggested answers or completions. Select the one that BEST answers the question or completes the statement. *PRINT THE LETTER OF THE CORRECT ANSWER IN THE SPACE AT THE RIGHT.*

Questions 1-10.

DIRECTIONS: Questions 1 through 10 are to be answered on the basis of the following information.

Fifty-year-old George Hoffman works in the basement of a garment factory. All of a sudden, he starts losing consciousness. An ambulance is called, and he is taken to the emergency room of the nearest hospital.

During the initial examination in the emergency room, he is found to have rapid, shallow breathing, non-palpable pulses over major vessels, and absent heart sounds.

1. Of the following, the MOST likely nursing diagnosis for this patient is

    A. arteriosclerosis
    B. cardiopulmonary arrest
    C. restrictive cardiomyopathy
    D. endocarditis

2. The nursing intervention of HIGHEST priority after receiving George in the emergency room would be

    A. to administer dopamine and norepinephrine to treat for shock
    B. to administer calcium chloride to help heartbeat
    C. defibrillation
    D. CPR

3. All of the following would be part of George's drug therapy EXCEPT

    A. lidocaine and procainamide
    B. epinephrine
    C. penicillin G
    D. sodium bicarbonate

4. While assessing George, the nurse probably does NOT expect to notice

    A. pallor
    B. dilation of pupils
    C. ventricular fibrillation
    D. petechiae and edema

5. George is unconscious. In an unconscious person, the relaxed tongue and neck muscles fail to lift the tongue from the posterior pharyngeal wall, blocking the hypo-pharyngeal airway. The nurse applies a basic head tilt maneuver to open the patient's airway, but does not receive a positive response.
Additional measures which may then be used by the nurse to open the airway include

    A. head tilt-chin lift
    B. head tilt-neck lift
    C. mandibular jaw thrust
    D. all of the above

69

6. George is also found to have suffered cervical spine injury as a result of falling. The nurse should know that _____ is absolutely contra-indicated in the presence of cervical spine injury.

 A. direct current defibrillation
 B. external cardiac compression
 C. backward head tilt
 D. all of the above

7. In single-rescuer CPR, the nurse would give 2 breaths (1 to 1.5 sec. each) after each cycle of _____ cardiac compressions, delivered at a rate of 80 to 100/minute.

 A. 5 B. 10 C. 15 D. 20

8. All of the following would be important and appropriate nursing interventions to save George's life EXCEPT:

 A. Begin precordial thump and, if successful, administer calcium chloride
 B. If precordial thump is unsuccessful, perform defibrillation
 C. If defibrillation is unsuccessful, initiate CPR immediately
 D. Assist with administration of and monitor effects of additional emergency drugs

9. In 2-rescuer CPR, one ventilation (1.5 to 2 sec.) should be given after each cycle of _____ cardiac compressions, delivered at a rate of 80 to 100/minute.

 A. 5 B. 10 C. 15 D. 20

10. Which of the following drugs is used as the standard therapy for ventricular fibrillation (VF) or ventricular tachycardia (VT), and is used with countershock to convert VF?

 A. Procainamide B. Bretylium tosylate
 C. Lidocaine   D. Epinephrine

Questions 11-20.

DIRECTIONS: Questions 11 through 20 are to be answered on the basis of the following information.

52-year-old John Goodman is brought to the emergency room by his wife with complaints of fever, cough, upper quadrant pain, and joint pain. Mrs. Goodman informs the health care team that John has also been losing weight.

11. John has been diagnosed with infective endocarditis. Mrs. Goodman has no knowledge about this disease, so she anxiously asks the nurse about it.
The nurse explains to Mrs. Goodman that infective endocarditis is a(n)

 A. inflammation of the parietal pericardium caused by a viral infection
 B. accumulation of fluid in the pericardium that prevents adequate ventricular filling, caused by a fungal infection
 C. microbial infection of the endocardium which may result in valvular incompetence or obstruction, myocardial abscess, or mycotic aneurysm
 D. formation of platelet and fibrin thrombi on cardiac valves and the adjacent endocardium in response to bacterial infection

12. Which of the following bacterias is among the common causes of infection in endocarditis?

    A. S. aureus
    B. S. viridans
    C. B. hemolytic streptococcus and gonococcus
    D. All of the above

13. While assessing John, the nurse expects to find all of the following EXCEPT

    A. malaise and fatigue
    B. edema
    C. elevated WBC and ESR
    D. increased Hgb and Hct

14. As a clinical manifestation, the symptom found in John that is NOT secondary to emboli is _____ pain.

    A. upper left quadrant
    B. flank
    C. joint
    D. chest

15. All of the following medications will be part of John's drug therapy EXCEPT

    A. epinephrine, to enhance endocardial contractile force
    B. antibiotics specific to the sensitivity of the organism cultured
    C. penicillin G and streptomycin, if the organism is not known
    D. antipyretics

16. In order for John to maintain homeostasis and avoid complications over long-term hospitalization, the one of the following things a nurse does NOT have to do is

    A. administer antibiotics as ordered
    B. control temperature elevation by administration of antipyretics
    C. evaluate for complications of emboli and congestive heart failure
    D. record baseline blood pressure in three positions, i.e., lying, sitting, and standing, in both arms

17. To isolate the etiologic agent, the nurse would perform _____ blood cultures of _____ mL each within 24 hours.

    A. 1 to 3; 10 to 20
    B. 3 to 5; 20 to 30
    C. 5 to 7; 10 to 20
    D. 3 to 5; 15 to 20

18. All of the following factors are associated with poor prognosis of infective endocarditis EXCEPT

    A. heart failure
    B. delay in initiating therapy
    C. young age
    D. major embolic events

19. Even after successful antimicrobial therapy, John will be at risk of sterile emboli and valve rupture for

    A. 6 months
    B. 1 year
    C. 1 1/2 years
    D. 2 years

20. John has recovered and is now ready to be discharged from the hospital. While discussing discharge planning, the nurse would instruct John and his wife regarding all of the following EXCEPT

   A. types of procedures or treatments that increase the chances of recurrence
   B. antifungal therapy, including name, purpose, dose, frequency, and side effects
   C. signs and symptoms of recurrent endocarditis
   D. avoidance of individuals with known infections

Questions 21-30.

DIRECTIONS: Questions 21 through 30 are to be answered on the basis of the following information.

54-year-old Donna Smith is brought to the hospital's emergency room by her husband after having fever, malaise, and chest pain aggravated by breathing and swallowing.

21. After being examined by the physician, Donna is diagnosed with pericarditis. Mr. Smith asks the nurse about the nature of this disease.
The nurse tells him that pericarditis is

   A. an accumulation of fluid or blood in the pericardium that prevents adequate ventricular filling, caused by a fungal infection
   B. an inflammation of the visceral and parietal pericardium, caused by a bacterial, viral, or fungal infection
   C. the formation of platelet and fibrin thrombi on cardiac valves and the adjacent pericardium in response to bacterial infection
   D. none of the above

22. Acute pericarditis may be a manifestation of all of the following EXCEPT

   A. rheumatoid arthritis
   B. systemic lupus erythematosus
   C. hemochromatosis
   D. scleroderma

23. Commonly used drugs that may produce acute pericarditis do NOT include

   A. procainamide   B. hydralazine
   C. isoniazid   D. lidocaine

24. Common causes of pericarditis include

   A. tuberculosis
   B. streptococcal infections
   C. staphylococcal infection
   D. all of the above

25. A scratchy, leathery sound heard in both systole and diastole is the CLASSIC sign of acute pericarditis known as

   A. pericardial friction rub
   B. epicardial rub friction
   C. myocardial friction rub
   D. dip and plateau

26. During Donna's assessment, the nurse does NOT expect to notice

   A. cough and hemoptysis
   B. tachycardia and pulsus paradoxus
   C. cyanosis or pallor
   D. decreased WBC and ESR

27. Which of the following is INCORRECT regarding Donna's drug therapy? It

   A. is medication for pain relief
   B. includes corticosteroids, salicylates, and indometha-cin
   C. includes calcium chloride
   D. is specific antibiotic therapy against the causative organism

28. The FALSE statement regarding chronic pericarditis is:

   A. It may be serous, fibrous, adhesive, hemorrhagic, purulent, fibrinous, or calcific
   B. It is asymptomatic unless constrictive pericarditis is present
   C. Coagulants are usually contraindicated in pericardial disease
   D. As a general treatment, meperidine 50 to 100 mg orally or IM may be given q 4 hours for pain

29. All of the following are proper nursing interventions to control Donna's condition EXCEPT

   A. ensuring comfort: bedrest with semi or high-Fowler's position
   B. monitoring hemodynamic parameters carefully
   C. administering medications as ordered and monitoring effects
   D. assessing for vascular complications

30. Donna has recovered and is now ready to be discharged. During the discharge planning conference, the nurse would probably NOT advise Mr. and Mrs. Smith about

   A. signs and symptoms of pericarditis indicative of a recurrence
   B. medication regimen including name, purpose, dosage, frequency, and side effects
   C. keeping all the emergency medications available at all times
   D. none of the above

KEY (CORRECT ANSWERS)

1.	B		16.	D
2.	D		17.	B
3.	C		18.	C
4.	D		19.	B
5.	D		20.	B
6.	C		21.	B
7.	C		22.	C
8.	A		23.	D
9.	A		24.	D
10.	C		25.	A
11.	C		26.	D
12.	D		27.	C
13.	D		28.	C
14.	C		29.	D
15.	A		30.	A

TEST 2

DIRECTIONS: Each question or incomplete statement is followed by several suggested answers or completions. Select the one that BEST answers the question or completes the statement. *PRINT THE LETTER OF THE CORRECT ANSWER IN THE SPACE AT THE RIGHT.*

Questions 1-10.

DIRECTIONS: Questions 1 through 10 are to be answered on the basis of the following information.

52-year-old Tim Brown visits his doctor after suffering for the last 3 days from pain in his legs and feet and numbness and tingling of the toes, and noticing shiny and taut skin with hair loss on his lower legs.

1. After being examined by the physician, Tim is diagnosed with arteriosclerosis obliterans. The nurse, after being asked by Tim about the disease, explains to him that arteriosclerosis obliterans is a chronic occlusive _____ disease that may affect the _____ .

    A. arterial; inferior vena cava or the extremities
    B. venous; superior vena cava or the extremities
    C. venous; pulmonary vessels or the extremities
    D. arterial; abdominal aorta or the lower extremities

2. The obstruction of blood flow with resultant ischemia usually does NOT affect the _____ artery.

    A. femoral   B. aortal
    C. oesophageal   D. iliac

3. Arteriosclerosis obliterans occurs MOST often in _____ ages _____ .

    A. men; 40-50   B. women; 40-50
    C. men; 50-60   D. women; 50-60

4. Which of the following is NOT a risk factor for arteriosclerosis obliterans?

    A. Hypotension   B. Cigarette smoking
    C. Hyperlipidemia   D. Diabetes mellitus

5. While assessing Mr. Brown, the nurse expects to notice all of the following EXCEPT

    A. both intermittent claudication and rest pain
    B. pallor after 1-2 minutes of elevating feet
    C. diminished or absent radial pulse
    D. diminished or absent dorsalis pedis pulse

6. The one of the following that is NOT a diagnostic test for arteriosclerosis obliterans is

    A. oscillometry   B. seriology
    C. angiography   D. doppler ultrasound

75

7. Mr. Brown is tired of staying in his bed and wants to walk around. The nurse's BEST advice for him would be that he can

   A. not do any physical activity until he is completely recovered and discharged from the hospital
   B. leave his bed not more than once a day
   C. leave his bed twice a day but not leave the room
   D. leave his bed 3-4 times a day and walk twice a day

8. All of the following would be appropriate nursing interventions for Mr. Brown's recovery EXCEPT to

   A. assess for sensory function and trophic changes
   B. encourage slow, progressive physical activity
   C. order medications as required
   D. protect the patient from injury

9. Which of the following would NOT be appropriate teaching and discharge planning for the nurse to provide to Mr. Brown?
   The importance of

   A. a restricted kcal, high-saturated fat diet
   B. continuing with established exercise program
   C. avoiding constrictive clothing and standing in any position for a long time
   D. foot care, immediately taking care of cuts, wounds, and injuries

10. Doppler ultrasound is the most widely used method in arteriosclerosis obliterans. The SIMPLEST method for estimating blood flow to the lower extremities is to measure the _____ blood pressure at the level of the ankle and compare it to the _____ pressure.

    A. systolic; brachial diastolic
    B. diastolic; brachial diastolic
    C. systolic; brachial systolic
    D. systolic; femoral systolic

Questions 11-19.

DIRECTIONS: Questions 11 through 19 are to be answered on the basis of the following information.

32-year-old George Dawson visits the hospital after continuously experiencing coldness, tingling, numbness, and burning in all his extremities and, lately, getting an ulceration in one of his digits. Mr. Dawson is also a cigarette smoker.

11. After being examined by the physician, Mr. Dawson is diagnosed with thromboangiitis obliterans.
    Thromboangiitis obliterans is BEST defined as an

    A. acute, inflammatory disorder affecting small size arteries of the lower extremities
    B. obliterative disease characterized by inflammatory changes in medium sized veins of the lower extremities
    C. acute, inflammatory disorder affecting large sized arteries of the lower extremities
    D. obliterative disease characterized by inflammatory changes in small and medium sized arteries and veins

12. The symptoms and signs of thromboangiitis obliterans are those of arterial ischemia and of superficial phlebitis. A history of migratory phlebitis, usually in the veins of the foot or leg, is present in _____ % of cases.

    A. 20   B. 30   C. 40   D. 50

13. Thromboangiitis obliterans occurs MOST often in _____ ages _____.

    A. men; 35-50
    B. women; 35-50
    C. men; 25-40
    D. women; 25-40

14. While assessing Mr. Dawson, the nurse expects to find all of the following EXCEPT

    A. intermittent claudication
    B. an increased posterior tibial pulse
    C. trophic changes
    D. ulceration and gangrene

15. _____ is NOT a diagnostic test for thromboangiitis obliterans.

    A. Angiography
    B. Contrast venography
    C. Oscillometry
    D. Doppler ultrasound

16. Which of the following would NOT be included among the appropriate nursing interventions to control Mr. Dawson's disease?

    A. Prepare the patient for surgery when required
    B. Provide vasodilators and analgesics as ordered
    C. Administer coagulants not more than once a day
    D. All of the above

17. All of the following are appropriate teaching and discharge information which should be provided by the nurse to Mr. Dawson EXCEPT the

    A. drug regimen, including names, dosages, frequency, and side effects
    B. need to avoid trauma to the affected extremity
    C. need to avoid heat and have a good airconditioner in the bedroom
    D. importance of stopping smoking

18. The only REALLY effective treatment for thromboangiitis obliterans is

    A. antibiotics
    B. corticosteroids
    C. anticoagulants
    D. cessation of smoking

19. In thromboangiitis obliterans, since the adventitia is usually more extensively infiltrated with fibroblasts, older lesions show periarterial fibrosis, which may involve the adjacent

    A. artery
    B. vein
    C. nerve
    D. all of the above

Questions 20-30.

DIRECTIONS: Questions 20 through 30 are to be answered on the basis of the following information.

30 year-old Sara Johnson got married six years ago. She never became pregnant, having used oral contraceptives. Now she visits the hospital after experiencing anxiety, fever, and chest pain.

20. After being examined by the physician, she is diagnosed with pulmonary embolism, which is BEST described as a(n)

   A. embolic obstruction to blood flow increasing venous pressure in the pulmonary artery and pulmonary hypotension
   B. embolic obstruction to blood flow involving the upper lobes of the lung because of higher blood flow
   C. lodgement of a blood clot in a pulmonary artery with subsequent obstruction of blood supply to the lung parenchyma
   D. lodgement of a blood clot in a pulmonary vein with subsequent obstruction of blood supply to the lung parenchyma

21. MOST pulmonary emboli arise as detached portions of venous thrombi formed in the

   A. deep veins of the legs
   B. right side of the heart
   C. pelvic area
   D. all of the above

22. Once released into the venous circulation, emboli are distributed to both lungs in about _____ % of cases, to the right lung in _____ % of cases, and to the left lung in _____ % of cases.

   A. 45; 40; 30
   B. 55; 30; 20
   C. 65; 20; 10
   D. 75; 10; 5

23. _____ lobes are involved in pulmonary embolism _____ times more often than _____ lobes.

   A. lower; 2; upper
   B. upper; 2; lower
   C. lower; 4; upper
   D. upper; 4; lower

24. Which of the following is NOT a risk factor for Mrs. Johnson?

   A. Trauma
   B. Pregnancy
   C. Oral contraceptives
   D. Intrauterine contraceptive devices

25. While assessing Mrs. Johnson, the nurse expects to notice all of the following EXCEPT

   A. severe dyspnea and a feeling of impending doom
   B. tachypnea and bradycardia
   C. increased pH due to hyperventilation
   D. crackles due to intensified pulmonic S_2

26. Concerning the diagnosis of pulmonary embolism, it is NOT correct that

   A. pulmonary arteriography reveals location and/or extent of embolism
   B. lung scan reveals adequacy or inadequacy of pulmonary circulation
   C. clinical symptoms and signs should suggest the diagnosis
   D. none of the above

27. All of the following drugs would be used in drug therapy for Mrs. Johnson EXCEPT   27._____

    A. anticoagulants
    B. dextran 70 to decrease viscosity and aggregation of blood cells
    C. narcotics for pain relief
    D. vasodepressors in the presence of shock

28. The surgical procedure used for the correction of pulmonary embolism is known as   28._____

    A. pulmonary thrombolectomy
    B. cardiac embolectomy
    C. pulmonary embolectomy
    D. cardiac thrombolectomy

29. It would be appropriate for the nurse attending to Mrs. Johnson to do all of the following EXCEPT   29._____

    A. administer oxygen therapy to correct hypoxemia
    B. provide adequate hydration to prevent hypocoagulability
    C. elevate the head of the bed to relieve dyspnea
    D. assist with turning, coughing, deep breathing, and passive ROM exercises

30. Which of the following is NOT considered among the appropriate teaching and discharge planning provided by the nurse to Mrs. Johnson?   30._____

    A. Use of plastic stockings when ambulatory
    B. Need to avoid sitting or standing for long periods of time
    C. Drug regimen
    D. Gradually increase walking distance

KEY (CORRECT ANSWERS)

1.	D	16.	C
2.	C	17.	C
3.	C	18.	D
4.	A	19.	D
5.	C	20.	C
6.	B	21.	D
7.	D	22.	C
8.	C	23.	C
9.	A	24.	D
10.	C	25.	B
11.	D	26.	D
12.	C	27.	D
13.	C	28.	C
14.	B	29.	B
15.	B	30.	A

EXAMINATION SECTION
TEST 1

DIRECTIONS: Each question or incomplete statement is followed by several suggested answers or completions. Select the one that BEST answers the question or completes the statement. *PRINT THE LETTER OF THE CORRECT ANSWER IN THE SPACE AT THE RIGHT.*

Questions 1-10.

DIRECTIONS: Questions 1 through 10 are to be answered on the basis of the following information.

Newly delivered, 34-year-old Susan Robinson comes to the hospital after feeling pain and noticing swollen, dilated, and tortuous skin veins in her lower extremities.

1. The physican examines Mrs. Robinson and makes a diagnosis of varicose veins, which is BEST described as elongated, dilated, tortuous superficial veins whose valves _____ , the condition occurring most often in the _____.

    A. are congenitally absent; lower extremities
    B. are scant; upper extremities
    C. have become incompetent; trunk
    D. are congenitally absent, scant, or have become incompetent; lower extremities and trunk

1.____

2. Varicose veins are MOST commonly found in _____ ages _____.

    A. women; 40 to 60
    B. men; 40 to 60
    C. women; 30 to 50
    D. both men and women; 30 to 50

2.____

3. All of the following are known to be predisposing factors for varicose veins EXCEPT

    A. congenital weakness of the veins
    B. obesity
    C. liver disease
    D. pregnancy

3.____

4. While assessing Mrs. Robinson, the nurse will NOT expect to notice

    A. pain after prolonged standing
    B. pain relieved by elevation
    C. tortuous skin veins
    D. deep, swollen and dilated veins

4.____

5. Which of the following would be used as a diagnostic test for Mrs. Robinson?

    A. X-rays
    B. Venography
    C. Plethysmography
    D. The Trendelenburg test

5.____

81

6. The one of the following that is NOT considered among the treatments for varicose veins is

   A. venography
   B. vein ligation
   C. injection sclerotherapy
   D. lightweight compression hosiery for small, mildly symptomatic varicose veins

7. All of the following would be appropriate nursing interventions for Mrs. Robinson EXCEPT

   A. measuring the circumference of the ankle and calf at least every 8 hours
   B. elevating legs above heart level
   C. applying knee-length elastic stockings
   D. providing adequate rest

8. It would NOT be an appropriate nursing intervention for vein ligation to

   A. keep the affected extremity above the level of the heart to prevent edema
   B. apply elastic bandages and stockings, which should be removed every 4 hours for short periods and reap-plied
   C. assist the patient out of bed within 24 hours, ensuring that elastic stockings are applied
   D. assess for increased bleeding, particularly in the groin area

9. Which of the following would NOT be part of the teaching and discharge planning provided by the nurse to Mrs. Robinson?
   Instruction regarding the

   A. importance of planned rest periods with elevation of the feet
   B. importance of adequate hydration to prevent hyper-coagulability
   C. need to avoid crossing the legs at the knees
   D. use of elastic stockings when on bed rest

10. All of the following statements about *spider veins* are correct EXCEPT:

    A. They are fine, intracutaneous angiectases of no serious consequence, but may be extensive and unsightly
    B. They are mostly symptomatic with patients' common complaints of burning and pain
    C. They can usually be eliminated by intracapillary injections of 1% solution of sodium tetradecyl sulfate through a fine-bore needle
    D. Best results are obtained by treating the whole leg at the initial visit and applying a compression bandage on the leg with ambulation for at least 3 weeks after treatment

Questions 11-18.

DIRECTIONS: Questions 11 through 18 are to be answered on the basis of the following information.

35-year-old Linda Gray comes to the hospital emergency room complaining of dizziness, weakness, and cold sensitivity after having excessive menses.

11. After a careful examination by the physician, Mrs. Gray is diagnosed with iron-deficiency anemia.
    Which of the following statements does NOT provide correct information about this disease?

    A. This is a chronic, microcytic, hypochromic anemia caused by either inadequate absorption or excessive loss of iron.
    B. Acute or chronic bleeding is the principal cause in adults resulting chiefly from trauma, excessive menses, and gastrointestinal bleeding.
    C. It can be caused by chronic diarrhea, malabsorption syndromes, and high cereal product intake with high animal protein ingestion.
    D. In iron-deficiency states, iron stores are depleted first, followed by a reduction in Hgb formation.

11.____

12. The incidence of iron-deficiency anemia is related to

    A. geographic location
    B. economic class
    C. age group and sex
    D. all of the above

12.____

13. The population affected MOST frequently by iron-deficiency anemia is

    A. women between ages 20-50
    B. men between ages 25-55
    C. children of all ages
    D. women between ages 15-45 and children

13.____

14. While assessing Mrs. Gray, the nurse expects to notice all of the following EXCEPT

    A. palpitations, dizziness, and cold sensitivity
    B. brittleness of hair and nails and pallor
    C. dysphagia, pruritis, and atrophic glossitis
    D. dyspnea and weakness

14.____

15. Which of the following is NOT a correct laboratory finding for iron-deficiency anemia?

    A. Red blood cells small (microcytic) and pale (hypo-chromic)
    B. Hemosiderin absent from bone marrow
    C. Hgb markedly decreased
    D. Reticulocyte count increased

15.____

16. All of the following would be appropriate nursing interventions for Mrs. Gray EXCEPT:

    A. Monitoring for signs and symptoms of bleeding through a hematest of pulmonary contents
    B. Providing for adequate rest and planning activities so as not to overtire
    C. Providing a thorough explanation of all diagnostic tests used to determine sources of possible bleeding, as it helps allay anxiety and ensure cooperation
    D. Monitoring for signs and symptoms of bleeding through a hematest of stool, urine, and gastric contents

16.____

17. It would NOT be an appropriate nursing intervention regarding oral iron preparations to

   A. use oral iron preparations as the route of choice, recommended to be given following meals or a snack
   B. dilute liquid preparations well and administer them using a straw to prevent staining teeth
   C. administer with orange juice when possible, as vitamin C (ascorbic acid) enhances iron absorption
   D. warn the patient that iron preparations will make stool color darker and may cause diarrhea

18. Concerning the use of parenteral iron preparations, do NOT

   A. use them in patients intolerant to oral preparations, patients who have no complaints with therapy, or patients who have continuing blood losses
   B. use one needle to withdraw and another to administer iron preparations, as tissue staining and irritation are problems
   C. use the Y track injection technique to prevent leakage into tissues
   D. massage the injection site, but encourage ambulation, as this will enhance absorption; advise against vigorous exercise and constricting garments

Questions 19-30.

DIRECTIONS: Questions 19 through 30 are to be answered on the basis of the following information.

58-year-old John Lithgow is brought to the hospital by his wife after suffering from weakness, sore mouth, diarrhea, and jaundice.

19. After being carefully examined by the physician, John is diagnosed with pernicious anemia, which is correctly explained by all of the following statements EXCEPT:

   A. It is a chronic, progressive, macrocytic anemia caused by a deficiency of intrinsic factor; the result is abnormally large erythrocytes and hypo-chlorhydria
   B. It is characterized by neurologic and gastrointestinal symptoms; death usually results if it goes untreated
   C. A lack of intrinsic factor is caused by gastric mucosal atrophy, possibly due to heredity, prolonged iron deficiency, or an autoimmune disorder
   D. It can result in patients who have had a total gastrec-tomy if vitamin B_2 is not administered

20. It is NOT a true pathophysiological finding about pernicious anemia that

   A. an intrinsic factor is necessary for the absorption of vitamin B_{12} by the large intestine
   B. b_{12} deficiency diminishes DNA synthesis, which results in defective maturation of cells, particularly rapidly dividing cells such as blood cells and gastrointestinal tract cells
   C. B_{12} deficiency can alter structure and function of peripheral nerves
   D. B_{12} deficiency can alter structure and function of the spinal cord and the brain

21. While assessing John, the nurse may expect to notice all of the following EXCEPT   21._____

    A. pallor, dyspnea, palpitations, and fatigue
    B. sore mouth with smooth, beefy, red tongue
    C. tingling, paresthesias of hands and feet and paralysis
    D. depression, hypertension, and psychosis

22. The one of the following that will NOT show up on a laboratory test of pernicious anemia is   22._____

    A. decreased erythrocyte count
    B. blood smear showing oval, macrocytic erythrocytes with a proportionate amount of Hgb
    C. very small numbers of reticulocytes in the blood following parenteral vitamin B_{12} administration
    D. elevated serum LDH

23. Which of the following statements is NOT true about the positive Schilling test? It   23._____

    A. measures absorption of radioactive vitamin B_{12} before parenteral administration of intrinsic factor
    B. measures absorption of radioactive vitamin B_{12} after parenteral administration of extrinsic factor
    C. is a definitive test for pernicious anemia
    D. is used to detect lack of intrinsic factor

24. All of the following will be part of John's drug therapy EXCEPT   24._____

    A. monthly maintenance by vitamin B_{12} injections
    B. iron preparations if Hgb level is inadequate to meet increased number of erythrocytes
    C. folic acid
    D. folic acid, which is safe if given in large amounts in addition to vitamin B_{12}

25. A 1000 mg injection of vitamin B_{12} can be given IM _____ times per week until hematologic abnormalities are corrected; then it is given once monthly.   25._____

    A. 2   B. 3
    C. 4   D. all of the above

26. A nurse should provide all of the following to control John's condition EXCEPT   26._____

    A. mouth care before and after meals using a hard toothbrush for better cleansing and non-irritating rinses
    B. a nutritious diet high in iron, protein, and vitamins such as fish, meat, milk/milk products, and eggs
    C. teaching concerning dietary instructions and the importance of lifelong vitamin B_{12} therapy
    D. bedrest if anemia is severe

27. Folic acid administration to anyone in the B_{12}-deprived state is contraindicated since it may result in fulminant _____ deficit.

   A. renal
   B. hepatic
   C. neurologic
   D. all of the above

28. Pernicious anemia MOST commonly occurs in

   A. men over age 50
   B. women over age 50
   C. blue-eyed persons of Scandinavian descent
   D. all of the above

29. Which of the following statements is FALSE about the Schilling test?

   A. Schilling III can be done after a 2-week trial of oral tetracycline.
   B. Labeled urine collection will contain less than 9% of the administered dose.
   C. Decreased excretion of radiolabeled B_{12} and normal excretion of labeled B_{12} bound to intrinsic factor establishes a defect in intrinsic factor production.
   D. Since the test provides 612 repletion, it should be performed after completion of all studies and planned therapeutic trials.

30. Which of the following is NOT considered a correct laboratory diagnosis finding for pernicious anemia?

   A. The anemia is macrocytic, with an MCV less than 100.
   B. In general, low values of less than 150 pg/mL are reliable indications of vitamin B_{12} deficiency.
   C. In borderline circumstances, i.e., 150-250 pg/mL, clinical judgment and other tests must supplement the radioassay.
   D. Autoantibodies to gastric parietal cells can be identified in 80 to 90% of patients with pernicious anemia and antibodies to intrinsic factor can be found in the sera of most of these patients.

KEY (CORRECT ANSWERS)

1.	D	16.	A
2.	D	17.	D
3.	C	18.	C
4.	D	19.	D
5.	D	20.	A
6.	A	21.	D
7.	A	22.	C
8.	B	23.	B
9.	D	24.	D
10.	B	25.	D
11.	C	26.	A
12.	D	27.	C
13.	D	28.	D
14.	C	29.	B
15.	D	30.	A

TEST 2

DIRECTIONS: Each question or incomplete statement is followed by several suggested answers or completions. Select the one that BEST answers the question or completes the statement. *PRINT THE LETTER OF THE CORRECT ANSWER IN THE SPACE AT THE RIGHT.*

1. In which of the following groups of people is stomach cancer MOST frequently found?   1.____
   - A. Spanish
   - B. Japanese
   - C. White Americans
   - D. Black Americans

2. A patient who is severely allergic to penicillin has streptococcal pharyngitis. The drug of choice is   2.____
   - A. vancomycin
   - B. tetracyline
   - C. erythromycin
   - D. sulfonamide

3. A 20-year-old male has gonococcal urethritis proven by a culture. The drug of choice to treat him is   3.____
   - A. penicillin
   - B. erythromycin
   - C. ceftriaxon
   - D. sulfonamide

4. Hookworm disease can be prevented by   4.____
   - A. inspecting meat
   - B. washing hands
   - C. sterilizing water supply
   - D. wearing shoes

5. Pulmonary fibrosis is an adverse side effect of the anti-cancer medication   5.____
   - A. adriamycin
   - B. vincristin
   - C. cyclophosphomide
   - D. bleomycin

6. A 25-year-old male is treated with methecillin for staphy-lococcus infection. Ten days later, the patient develops hematuria. The MOST likely diagnosis is   6.____
   - A. membrano proliferative glomerulonephritis
   - B. acute glomerulonephritis
   - C. nephrotic syndrome
   - D. allergic nephritis

7. A 20-year-old male's exudative tonsilopharyngitis was treated with ampicillin, after which he developed generalized rash and hepatosplenomaly. What is the MOST likely diagnosis?   7.____
   - A. Infectious mononucleosis
   - B. Diphtheria
   - C. Streptococcal pharyngitis
   - D. Hemophilus influenzae pharyngitis

8. A 25-year-old woman has vaginal discharge and her vaginal culture is positive for chlamydia.
The treatment of choice is

    A. penicillin
    B. metronidazol
    C. erythromycin
    D. amphotericin B

8.____

Questions 9-17.

DIRECTIONS: Questions 9 through 17 are to be answered on the basis of the following information.

Sixty-year-old James Bond is brought to the emergency room by his wife after suffering from severe low abdominal and low back pain.

9. After being examined by the physician, Mr. Bond is diagnosed with an abdominal aortic aneurysm, which is BEST defined as a

    A. saccular aneurysm developed above the renal arteries and caused by arteriosclerosis
    B. dissecting aneurysm developed below the iliac bifurcation and caused by atherosclerosis
    C. localized dilation of the aorta developing just above the iliac bifurcation caused by trauma
    D. localized dilation of the abdominal aorta developing just below the renal arteries but above the iliac bifurcation caused by arteriosclerosis, atherosclerosis, hypertension, trauma, syphilis, or other types of infectious processes

9.____

10. Abdominal aortic aneurysm occurs MOST often in _____ ages _____.

    A. men; 51-60
    B. women; 51-60
    C. men; 61 and over
    D. women; 61 and over

10.____

11. Abdominal aortic aneurysms of arteriosclerosis commonly pass unnoticed until they become large enough to cause symptoms or to be felt as a pulsating mass of about _____ cm.

    A. 2-4   B. 4-6   C. 6-8   D. 8-10

11.____

12. While assessing Mr. Bond, the nurse would expect to notice all of the following EXCEPT

    A. severe mid to low abdominal pain and low back pain
    B. mass in the periumbilical area or slightly to the left of the midline with bruits heard over the mass
    C. pulsating abdominal mass
    D. increased femoral pulses

12.____

13. _____ is(are) NOT used as a diagnostic test for an abdominal aortic aneurysm.

    A. X-rays
    B. Aortography
    C. Venography
    D. Ultrasound

13.____

14. Appropriate pre-operative nursing interventions for abdominal aortic aneurysms include   14.____

    A. preparing patient for surgery
    B. assessing rate and rhythm of peripheral pulses
    C. assessing character of the peripheral pulses
    D. all of the above

15. A nurse attending post-operatively to a patient with an abdominal aortic aneurysm does NOT have to   15.____

    A. make circulation checks noting rate, rhythm, and character of all pulses distal to the graft at least twice a day
    B. monitor hourly outputs through a Foley catheter
    C. keep the patient flat in bed without sharp flexion of the hip or knee
    D. prevent thrombophlebitis by encouraging the patient to dorsiflex his foot while in bed

16. All of the following would be part of the teaching and discharge planning provided by the nurse to Mr. Bond EXCEPT advice concerning the importance of   16.____

    A. changes in color or temperature of extremities
    B. avoidance of prolonged sitting, standing, and smoking
    C. a gradual progressive activity regimen
    D. adherence to a low cholesterol and a high-saturated fat diet

17. The MOST appropriate medical management for Mr. Bond's recovery would be   17.____

    A. injection sclerotherapy
    B. clinical monitoring of the indicators of shock
    C. surgical resection of the lesion and replacement with a graft
    D. chlorpromazine 10 to 25 mg orally q 6 to 8 hours

Questions 18-30.

DIRECTIONS: Questions 18 through 30 are to be answered on the basis of the following information.

48-year-old Marge Simpson has been working in a garment factory for the last ten years as a sewing machine operator 8 to 10 hours a day. She comes to the hospital after feeling pain and noticing tenderness and redness in one of her lower extremities. Marge is also a cigarette smoker.

18. After being examined by the physician, Marge is diagnosed with thrombophlebitis, which is BEST defined as the   18.____

    A. inflammation of the vessel walls of saphenous and femoral veins with formation of a thrombus
    B. inflammation of the walls of femoral and popliteal veins with formation of an embolus
    C. inflammation of the arterial wall with formation of a thrombus, the most frequently affected arteries being saphenous, femoral, and popliteal
    D. presence of a thrombus in a vein, most commonly in the saphenous, femoral, and popliteal veins

19. Which of the following factors may contribute to thrombophlebitis?

    A. Injury to the epithelium of the vein
    B. Hypercoagulability
    C. Stasis
    D. All of the above

20. The nurse knows that the terms phlegmasia alba dolens and phlegmesia cerulea dolens are applied to extensive thrombosis of the involved extremity depending on

    A. what part of the extremity is involved
    B. size of the involvement
    C. its color
    D. its temperature

21. Effort (strain) thrombosis occurs in the _____ veins, secondary to trauma to the vein in the thoracic outlet during unusual physical effort in which the arm is fully abducted.

    A. esophageal
    B. aortic
    C. subclavian
    D. pulmonary

22. The nurse would consider all of the following risk factors for Marge EXCEPT

    A. cigarette smoking
    B. intrauterine contraceptive devices
    C. prolonged immobility
    D. complications of surgery

23. The nurse, while assessing Marge, would NOT expect to notice

    A. tenderness, redness, and induration along the course of the vein in the situation of superficial vein involvement
    B. swelling, venous distension of the limb; tenderness and cyanosis in deep veins
    C. elevated WBC and decreased ESR
    D. positive Homan's sign in the situation of deep vein involvement

24. Regarding the anticoagulant therapy used for Marge, it is INCORRECT that

    A. heparin blocks the conversion of prothrombin to thrombin and reduces the formation or extension of thrombus
    B. side effects of heparin include spontaneous bleeding, ecchymosis, cyanosis, thrombocytopenia, and others
    C. warfarin (coumadin) blocks prothrombin synthesis by interfering with vitamin D synthesis
    D. side effects of warfarin include nausea and vomiting, diarrhea, urticaria, pruritis, transient hair loss, burning sensation of feet and others

25. All of the following are true concerning Marge's medical management by surgery EXCEPT:

    A. A good prognosis of vein ligation
    B. A contraindication of vein stripping
    C. Venous thrombectomy; removal of a clot in the ilio-femoral region
    D. Plication of the inferior vena cava; insertion of an umbrella-like prosthesis into the lumen of the vena cava to filter incoming clot

26. _____ would NOT be used as one of the diagnostic tests in the case of Marge.

    A. Venography
    B. Doppler ultrasonography
    C. Plethysmography
    D. The Trendelenburg test

27. A nurse treating Marge would NOT have to

    A. provide bedrest, elevating the involved extremity to increase venous return and decrease edema
    B. apply continuous warm, moist soaks to decrease lymphatic congestion
    C. assess vital signs every 8 hours
    D. monitor for chest pain or shortness of breath

28. When using heparin as an anticoagulant in thrombophlebitis, a nurse should do all of the following EXCEPT

    A. recognize that one of the proper injection techniques is the use of 26- or 27-gauge tuberculin syringe with 1/2 - 5/8 in. needle, injected into the fatty layer of the abdomen below the iliac crest
    B. monitor PTT; dosage should be adjusted to keep PTT between 1.5-2.5 times the normal control level
    C. assess for increased bleeding tendencies and instruct the patient to observe for and report these
    D. have an antidote (protamine sulfate) available

29. All of the following would be appropriate nursing interventions concerning use of warfarin (coumadin) as an anticoagulant in thrombophlebitis EXCEPT

    A. obtaining careful medication history, as there are many drug-drug interactions
    B. instructing patient to use a hard toothbrush and to floss regularly
    C. having an antidote (vitamin K) available
    D. instructing patient to wear Medic-Alert bracelet

30. It would NOT be appropriate teaching and discharge planning for the nurse to tell Marge to

    A. avoid prolonged standing or sitting, constrictive clothing, smoking, and oral contraceptives
    B. avoid physical activities, such as swimming
    C. maintain adequate hydration to prevent hypercoagability
    D. use of elastic stockings when ambulatory

KEY (CORRECT ANSWERS)

1.	B	16.	D
2.	C	17.	C
3.	C	18.	D
4.	D	19.	D
5.	D	20.	C
6.	D	21.	C
7.	A	22.	B
8.	C	23.	C
9.	D	24.	C
10.	C	25.	B
11.	B	26.	D
12.	D	27.	C
13.	C	28.	A
14.	D	29.	B
15.	A	30.	B

EXAMINATION SECTION
TEST 1

DIRECTIONS: Each question or incomplete statement is followed by several suggested answers or completions. Select the one that BEST answers the question or completes the statement. *PRINT THE LETTER OF THE CORRECT ANSWER IN THE SPACE AT THE RIGHT.*

Questions 1-10.

DIRECTIONS: Questions 1 through 10 are to be answered on the basis of the following information.

28-year-old Robert Davidson is brought to the hospital by his family members after having an elevated temperature for the last few days, continuous weight loss, and difficulty breathing. Robert also has a recent medical history of pneumonia.

1. After being carefully examined by the physician, Robert is diagnosed with acquired immune deficiency syndrome (AIDS).
   All of the following are true statements about this disorder EXCEPT:

   A. It is a secondary immunodeficiency syndrome caused by a virus and characterized by severe immune deficiency resulting in opportunistic infections, malignancies, and neurologic lesions in individuals without prior history of immunologic abnormality
   B. It results from infection with human immunodeficiency virus (HIV), an RNA virus that preferentially infects helper T-lymphocytes; it is transmissible through sexual contact, contaminated blood or blood products, and from an infected woman to her child in utero or through breastfeeding
   C. The HIV virus is present in an infected person's blood, semen, saliva, tears, vaginal secretions, and sweat
   D. Its epidemiology is similar to that of hepatitis B; increased incidence in populations in which sexual promiscuity is common and in IV drug abusers

1.____

2. While assessing Robert, the nurse may expect to notice all of the following EXCEPT

   A. AIDS-related complex: nonspecific symptoms such as fatigue, weakness, anorexia, diarrhea, weight loss, pallor, fever, and night sweats
   B. dyspnea and progressive hypoxemia secondary to neurologic lesion
   C. progressive weight loss secondary to diarrhea and a general wasting syndrome
   D. Temperature elevation which may be intermittent or persistent

2.____

3. Which of the following will NOT be an expected assessment finding in a patient with AIDS?

   A. Neurologic dysfunction secondary to acute meningitis, progressive dementia, encephalopathy, and encephalitis
   B. Presence of opportunistic infection, such as pneumocystis carinii pneumonia
   C. Presence of Herpes simplex, cytomegalovirus, and Epstein-Barr viruses
   D. Presence of oral or bronchial candidiasis

3.____

4. The nurse assessing Robert for neoplasms will NOT expect to notice

   A. Kaposi's sarcoma
   B. histiocytic lymphoma
   C. Burkitt's lymphoma
   D. diffuse undifferentiated non-Hodgkin's lymphoma

5. Transmission of HIV to another person requires transmission of body substances containing infected cells, e.g., blood or plasma. Uniquely, HIV can be expected to be present in any fluid or exudate that contains lymphocytes, e.g., in saliva, tears, semen, and vaginal secretions.
   Transmission of HIV by _____ has NOT been reported.

   A. plasma-containing fluids
   B. body secretions
   C. body excretions
   D. saliva and tears

6. Among persons with hemophilia, AIDS has now become the leading cause of mortality replacing

   A. intravascular coagulation
   B. thrombosis
   C. embolism
   D. hemorrhage

7. Which of the following is NOT considered a correct laboratory finding for an AIDS patient?

   A. Diagnosis based on clinical criteria and positive HIV antibody test, confirmed by western blot assay
   B. Thrombocytopenia and leukopenia with profound lymphopenia
   C. Anemia, and decreased circulatory T_4 lymphocyte cells
   D. High $T_4:T_8$ lymphocyte ratio

8. It would NOT be an appropriate nursing intervention to control Robert's condition to

   A. administer medications as ordered for concomitant disease and to monitor for signs of medication toxicity, including neutropenia and nephrotoxicity
   B. if leukopenia develops, institute precautions appropriate for an immunosuppressed patient
   C. keep him in a single room, avoid IV injections, and limit staff and visitors with upper respiratory or other active infections
   D. provide emotional support for the patient and significant others

9. All of the following are considered appropriate AIDS precautions EXCEPT

   A. gowns, masks, and gloves are necessarily required during contact with body fluids, blood, secretions, and excretions
   B. articles contaminated with blood, secretions, excretions, or body fluids are double-bagged
   C. articles contaminated with blood, secretions, excretions, or body fluids are washed thoroughly with 1:10 solution of household bleach and water

D. all laboratory specimens must be bagged and labeled

10. The teaching and discharge planning provided by the nurse to Robert would include information regarding

    A. communicability and routes of transmission, e.g., shared syringes and sexual intercourse, either vaginal, oral or anal
    B. use of condoms for sexual intercourse
    C. community resources, including support groups, local church groups, gay rights groups, and drug rehabilitation programs
    D. all of the above

Questions 11-17.

DIRECTIONS: Questions 11 through 17 are to be answered on the basis of the following information.

26-year-old David Spade is brought to the hospital by his parents after having headache and chilliness followed by high fever and sore throat.

11. After being examined by the physician, David is diagnosed with infectious mononucleosis.
    All of the following are correct features of this disease EXCEPT:

    A. It is an acute disease characterized clinically by high fever, sore throat, and generalized lymphadeno-pathy
    B. It is characterized pathologically by diffuse hyperplasia of lymphatic tissue; hematologically by an increase in lymphocytes, many of which are atypical; and serologically by development of persistent antibodies to the Epstein-Barr virus
    C. It most commonly affects adolescents and young adults
    D. The incubation period is 8 to 10 weeks

12. Infectious mononucleosis occurs ONLY in persons who have

    A. past medical history of the disease
    B. family history of the disease
    C. previously had no antibodies to the virus
    D. genetically inherited the disease

13. While assessing David, the nurse may expect to notice all of the following EXCEPT

    A. lethargy, sore throat, and tonsilitis
    B. enlarged spleen (splenomegaly is present in 50% of the patients)
    C. liver involvement (liver function tests are abnormal in almost all patients, hepatomegaly is noted in about 20% of the patients)
    D. jaundice (found in more than 15% of the patients)

14. _____ is NOT a diagnostic test for infectious mononucleosis.

    A. Lymphangiogram
    B. Hemogram
    C. Heterophil antibody test
    D. EBV-specific serodiagnostic tests

15. A CORRECT diagnostic test finding for infectious mononucleosis is _____, positive heterophil antibody, and _____, monospot tests.

   A. increased atypical WBCs; positive
   B. decreased typical WBCs; negative
   C. increased atypical RBCs; positive
   D. decreased typical RBCs; negative

16. Which of the following statements is NOT true about the treatment of infectious mononucleosis?

   A. Bedrest should be enforced during the acute phase of fever and malaise and prolonged in cases with hepatic involvement.
   B. Strenuous exercise must be avoided while the spleen is enlarged.
   C. Acetaminophen, rather than aspirin, should be used to control headache because of the rare association of EBV with Reye's Syndrome.
   D. Antibiotics are of important value unless secondary bacterial infection is present.

17. Treatment of infectious mononucleosis by _____ has shown a trend toward shorter duration of tonsilitis and pharyngitis and faster return to pre-illness weight, as compared to untreated controls.

   A. erythromycin   B. ampicillin
   C. intravenous acyclovir   D. oral acyclovir

Questions 18-24.

DIRECTIONS: Questions 18 through 24 are to be answered on the basis of the following information.

34-year-old John Taylor comes to the hospital after having dyspnea and difficulty breathing. He also notices brown pigmentation in his skin.

18. After being examined by the physician, John is diagnosed with aplastic anemia. Which of the following statements does NOT give correct information about this disease?

   A. Pancytopenia of granulocytes, platelets, and erythro-cyte production is due to fatty replacement of the bone marrow.
   B. Depression of serum LDH production is due to fatty replacement of the bone marrow.
   C. Bone marrow destruction may be idiopathic or secondary.
   D. Secondary aplastic anemia may be caused by chemical toxins, drugs, radiations, and immunologic injury.

19. Aplastic anemia is MOST common in

   A. adolescents and young adults
   B. women over age 45
   C. adolescents
   D. men over age 45

5 (#1)

20. While assessing John, the nurse expects to find all of the following EXCEPT   20.____

   A. fatigue and dyspnea
   B. hypertension
   C. increased susceptibility to infection
   D. bleeding tendencies and hemorrhage

21. All of the following would be considered correct laboratory findings in John,s case EXCEPT   21.____

   A. normocytic anemia
   B. granulocytopenia
   C. thrombocytopenia
   D. bone marrow biopsy showing that marrow is fatty and contains a lot of developing cells

22. The one of the following that will NOT be part of appropriate medical management for John is   22.____

   A. blood transfusions as a key to therapy until the patient,s own marrow begins to produce blood cells
   B. aggressive treatment of infections
   C. administration of corticosteroids to stimulate bone marrow function and to increase venous resistance, which is found to be more effective in adults than in children
   D. bone marrow transplantation

23. All of the following would be appropriate actions for a nurse to take to control John,s problem EXCEPT   23.____

   A. administer blood transfusions as ordered
   B. provide nursing care in the event of bone marrow transplantation
   C. encourage high-vitamin, low-protein diet to help reduce incidence of inflammation
   D. maintain neutropenic isolation

24. John is being monitored for signs of bleeding.   24.____
    Which of the following nursing measures will NOT minimize the risk of bleeding?

   A. Use a soft toothbrush and electric razor
   B. Encourage intramuscular injections
   C. Hematest urine and stool
   D. Observe for oozing from gums, petechiae, or ecchymoses

Questions 25-30.

DIRECTIONS: Questions 25 through 30 are to be answered on the basis of the following information.

34-year-old Denzel Malcolm comes to the hospital after having abdominal pain and nausea. He also has slight jaundice.

25. After being examined by the physician, Mr. Malcolm is diagnosed with hemolytic anemia, which is accurately described by all of the following statements EXCEPT:

    A. It is in a category of diseases in which there is an increased rate of red blood cell destruction
    B. It may be congenital, which includes hereditary spherocytosis, G_6PD deficiency, sickle cell anemia, and thalassemia
    C. It may be acquired, which includes transfusion incompatibilities, thrombotic thrombocytopenic purpura, disseminated intravascular clotting, and spur cell anemia
    D. The degree of anemia is determined by the lag between leukocyte hemolysis and the rate of bone marrow erythropoiesis

26. MOST hemolysis occurs extravascularly, i.e., in phagocytic cells of the

    A. spleen
    B. liver
    C. bone marrow
    D. all of the above

27. While assessing Mr. Malcolm, the nurse does NOT expect to notice

    A. pallor, scleral icterus, and slight jaundice
    B. chills, fever, irritability, precordial spasm and pain (acute)
    C. abdominal pain and nausea, vomiting, diarrhea, and melena
    D. hematuria, marked jaundice, and rapid breathing

28. Of the following, the one that is NOT considered a correct laboratory test finding in hemolytic anemia is

    A. decreased Hgb and Hct
    B. decreased reticulocyte count
    C. Coombs, test positive if autoimmune features are absent
    D. elevated unconjugated bilirubin fraction

29. All of the following would be appropriate nursing measures for medical management of Mr. Malcolm EXCEPT

    A. identification and, if possible, elimination of causative factors
    B. administration of ascorbic acid supplements
    C. blood transfusion therapy
    D. splenectomy

30. It would be appropriate for a nurse to do all of the following to control hemolytic anemia EXCEPT:

    A. In the presence of jaundice and associated pruritis, avoid soap during bathing and use hot water
    B. Monitor for signs and symptoms of hypoxia, including confusion, cyanosis, shortness of breath, tachycardia, and palpitations
    C. Note that the presence of jaundice may make assessment of skin color in hypoxia unreliable
    D. Maintain frequent turning and meticulous skin care as skin friability is increased

KEY (CORRECT ANSWERS)

1.	C	16.	D
2.	B	17.	C
3.	D	18.	B
4.	B	19.	A
5.	D	20.	B
6.	D	21.	D
7.	D	22.	C
8.	C	23.	C
9.	A	24.	B
10.	D	25.	D
11.	D	26.	D
12.	C	27.	D
13.	D	28.	C
14.	A	29.	B
15.	A	30.	A

TEST 2

DIRECTIONS: Each question or incomplete statement is followed by several suggested answers or completions. Select the one that BEST answers the question or completes the statement. *PRINT THE LETTER OF THE CORRECT ANSWER IN THE SPACE AT THE RIGHT.*

Questions 1-11.

DIRECTIONS: Questions 1 through 11 are to be answered on the basis of the following information.

6-year-old Rodney Stewart is brought to the hospital by his parents after having abdominal pain. They noticed an infection in one of his legs. Rodney has also been having some difficulty in urination.

1. After a careful examination by the physician, Rodney is diagnosed with sickle cell anemia, which is correctly characterized by all of the following EXCEPT

   A. autosomal recessive inheritance pattern
   B. individuals who are homozygous for the sickle cell gene have the disease, since more than 80% of their hemoglobin is abnormal (HgbS)
   C. the structure of hemoglobin is changed, i.e., the eighth rung of the beta chain changes glutamine for valine
   D. red blood cells live for 6-20 days instead of 120, causing hemolytic anemia

1.____

2. HgbS, which has reduced oxygen-carrying capacity, replaces all or part of the hemoglobin in the red blood cells. When oxygen is released, the shape of the red blood cells changes from

   A. round and pliable to oval and rigid
   B. oval and pliable to round and rigid
   C. crescent and rigid to round and pliable
   D. round and pliable to crescent and rigid

2.____

3. If Rodney comes through a situation of sickle cell crisis, which of the following will NOT be a correct statement about the same?

   A. Vaso-occlusive (thrombocytic) crisis is the most common type, where crescent-shaped red blood cells clump together and agglutination causes blockage of small blood vessels.
   B. In thrombocytic crisis, the blockage of small blood vessels causes the blood viscosity to increase, producing sludging and resulting in further hypoxia and increased sickling.
   C. The second type of crisis is splenic sequestration, which is often seen in toddlers and preschoolers where sickled cells block outflow tract, resulting in sudden and massive collection of sickled cells in the spleen.
   D. In splenic sequestration, the blockage of outflow tract leads to hypervolemia and a severe increase in blood pressure and hemoglobin, leading to shock.

3.____

102

4. While assessing Rodney, the nurse does NOT expect to notice

   A. splenomegaly, found initially due to hemolysis and phagocytosis, and later on due to fibrosis from repeated infarct to spleen
   B. weak bones or spinal defects, due to hyperplasia of marrow and osteoporosis
   C. frequent infections, especially with H. influenzae and D. pneumoniae
   D. leg ulcers, due to blockage of blood supply to major muscles of the leg

5. While assessing a patient of sickle cell anemia, the nurse may notice all of the following EXCEPT

   A. infants having dactylitis (hand-foot syndrome), a symmetrical painful soft tissue swelling of hands and feet in the absence of trauma
   B. delayed growth and development, especially a delay in sexual development
   C. hemosiderosis, as the cause of liver failure
   D. complaint of pain wherever vaso-occlusive crisis occurs

6. All of the following are correct regarding diagnostic tests for sickle cell anemia EXCEPT:

   A. Hgb indicates anemia, usually 6-9 gm/dL
   B. *Sickle Cell Test* is done by deoxygenation of a drop of blood on a slide with a cover slip. It takes 45-60 minutes for results to be read. False negatives for the trait are possible.
   C. In *Sickledex,* a drop of blood from a fingerstick is mixed with a solution and the mixture turns cloudy in the presence of HgbS. Results are available within a few minutes. False negatives in anemic patients or young infants are possible.
   D. *Hgb Electrophoresis* is a diagnostic for both the disease and the trait and provides accurate and fast results

7. The one of the following which is NOT part of an appropriate medical management for sickle cell anemia is

   A. administration of urea which interferes with hydrophobic bonds of the HgbS molecules; analgesics/ narcotics to control pain; and antibiotics to control infection
   B. exchange transfusions
   C. intravenous and intramuscular hydration
   D. splenectomy and bedrest

8. All of the following would be appropriate nursing interventions to control Rodney,s condition EXCEPT

   A. keeping the child well hydrated and oxygenated
   B. avoiding tight clothing that could impair circulation
   C. keeping wounds dry and clean
   D. providing bedrest to decrease energy expenditure and increase oxygen use

9. An INAPPROPRIATE nursing intervention for a patient of sickle cell anemia in crisis would be to

   A. correct metabolic acidosis
   B. among analgesics, avoid aspirin, as it enhances acidosis which promotes sickling, and anticoagulants as sludging is not due to clotting
   C. keep arms and legs from becoming warm
   D. test siblings for presence of sickle cell trait disease

10. The nurse would provide Rodney and his parents with teaching and discharge planning concerning all of the following EXCEPT 10.____

     A. to sew pads in knees and elbow of clothing
     B. pre-op teaching for splenectomy if needed
     C. genetic counseling
     D. need to avoid activities that interfere with oxygena-tion, such as mountain climbing and flying in unpressurized planes

11. A recent study demonstrated a marked reduction in the occurrence of pneumococcal septicemia in infants given _____ starting by age 4 months, suggesting that this should become standard procedure. 11.____

     A. penicillin   B. cephalosporin   C. tetracycline   D. erythromycin

Questions 12-19.

DIRECTIONS: Questions 12 through 19 are to be answered on the basis of the following information.

36 year-old Walter Reade is brought to the emergency room after having convulsions and petechiae and ecchymoses on his skin. Walter also has a recent history of bacterial infection from a gram-negative microorganism.

12. After being examined by the physician, Walter is diagnosed with disseminated intravascular coagulation (DIC), which is characterized by all of the following EXCEPT 12.____

     A. diffuse fibrin deposition within arterioles and capillaries with widespread coagulation all over the body, and subsequent depletion of clotting factors
     B. hemorrhage from kidneys, brain, adrenals, heart, and other organs
     C. patients are usually critically ill with an obstetric, surgical, hemolytic, or neoplastic disease
     D. may be linked with entry of thromboplastic substances into the lymph nodes

13. Which of the following is NOT a pathophysiological finding for DIC? 13.____

     A. Underlying disease, e.g., toxemia of pregnancy, cancer causes release of thromboplastic substances that promote the deposition of fibrin throughout the microcirculation.
     B. Microthrombi form in many organs causing microinfarcts and tissue necrosis; white blood cells are trapped in fibrin strands and hemolysed.
     C. Platelets, prothrombin, and other clotting factors are destroyed, leading to bleeding.
     D. Excessive clotting activates the fibrinolytic system, which inhibits platelet function, causing further bleeding.

14. While assessing Walter, the nurse may expect to notice all of the following EXCEPT 14.____

     A. petechiae and ecchymoses on the skin, hairs, mucous membranes, heart, lungs, and other organs
     B. prolonged bleeding from breaks in the skin, e.g., IV sites; severe and uncontrollable hemorrhage during surgical procedures
     C. oliguria and acute renal failure
     D. convulsions, coma, and death

15. _____ is NOT a correct laboratory finding for DIC.

   A. Prolonged PT
   B. Prolonged PTT
   C. Prolonged thrombin time
   D. Elevated fibrinogen level

16. All of the following laboratory findings indicate DIC EXCEPT

   A. depressed platelet count
   B. depressed fibrin split products
   C. depressed factor assays (II, V, VII)
   D. strongly positive protamine sulfate test

17. The INCORRECT statement regarding the treatment of DIC is:

   A. Identification and control of underlying disease is key
   B. Blood transfusions which include whole blood, packed red blood cells, platelets, plasma, cryoprecipitates, and volume expanders are used
   C. Heparin is usually indicated to stop intravascular coagulation if the underlying disorder can be brought under control quickly
   D. Heparin inhibits thrombin, thus preventing further clot formation, allowing coagulation factors to accumulate

18. A nurse treating a patient in Walter's condition would NOT be expected to

   A. monitor blood loss and attempt to quantify
   B. observe for signs of additional bleeding or thrombus formation, and monitor appropriate laboratory data
   C. administer blood transfusions and medications as ordered and teach patient the importance of avoiding aspirin or aspirin-containing compounds
   D. provide psychological counseling

19. Which of the following is NOT an appropriate nursing intervention to prevent any further injury in a patient of DIC?

   A. Recommend intramuscular injections rather than intravenous
   B. Apply pressure to bleeding sites
   C. Turn and position patient frequently and gently
   D. Provide frequent nontraumatic mouth care, e.g., soft toothbrush or gauze sponge

Questions 20-30.

DIRECTIONS: Questions 20 through 30 are to be answered on the basis of the following information.

52-year-old Sonny Crockett is brought to the hospital by his wife after having remarkable weakness, headache, fatigue, light-headedness, visual disturbances, and breathing problems. Mr. Crockett also complains of stomach burning.

20. After being carefully examined by the physician, Mr. Crockett is diagnosed with polycythemia vera (PV), which is BEST defined as a(n) _____ characterized by an increase in _____ .

   A. acute disorder of unknown cause; Hb concentration and red blood cell mass
   B. chronic myeloproliferative disorder; red blood cell mass (erythrocytosis)
   C. acute myeloproliferative disorder; red blood cell mass
   D. chronic myeloproliferative disorder of unknown cause; Hb concentration and red blood cell mass (erythrocytosis)

21. Regarding the incidence finding of polycythemia vera, it is TRUE that

   A. PV occurs in about 5 million persons, and more often in Jews and males, about 1.4:1
   B. at the time of diagnosis, the mean age is 60 years with a range from 15 to 90 years, but rarely in children
   C. 5% of patients are younger than 40 at onset
   D. all of the above

22. The etiology of PV tells us that

   A. the bone marrow sometimes appears normal but usually is hypercellular; hyperplasia involves all marrow elements and replaces marrow fat
   B. there is increased production and turnover of red blood cells, neutrophils, and platelets; increased megakaryocytes may be present in *clumps*
   C. marrow iron is absent in more than 90% of patients, even when phlebotomy has not been done
   D. all of the above

23. Which of the following is NOT considered a correct patho-physiological finding for polycythemia vera?

   A. A pronounced increase in the production of erythro-cytes accompanied by an increase in the production of myelocytes, leukocytes within bone marrow, and thrombocytes
   B. The consequences of this given overproduction are an increase in blood viscosity, an increase in total blood volume, i.e., 2-3 times greater than normal and severe congestion of all tissues and organs with blood
   C. Study of female patients with PV who are heterozygous at the X-chromosome-1inked locus for G6PD shows that red blood cells, granulocytes, and platelets all have different isoenzymes, supporting a clonal origin of this disorder at a pluripotent stem cell level. The cause of this proliferation is unknown.
   D. About 25% of patients have a reduction in red blood cell survival, with a failure to increase further erythropoiesis adequately; anemia and myelofibrosis develop. Extramedullary hematopoiesis takes place in the spleen, liver, and other sites with the potential for blood cell formation.

24. The nurse assessing Mr. Crockett may expect to notice all of the following EXCEPT

   A. ruddy complexion and duskiness of mucosa secondary to capillary congestion in the skin and mucous membranes
   B. hypertension associated with vertigo, headache, and *fullness* in the head secondary to increased blood volume
   C. symptoms of CHF secondary to overwork of the lungs
   D. thrombus formation: possible CVA, MI, gangrene of the extremities, DVT, and pulmonary embolism

25. The one of the following that is NOT an expected assessment finding for a patient of polycythemia vera is

   A. bleeding and hemorrhage secondary to congestion and overdistension of capillaries and venules
   B. hepatomegaly and splenomegaly
   C. Hunner's ulcer secondary to increased gastric secretions
   D. gout secondary to increased uric acid released by nucleoprotein breakdown

26. Increased _____ is NOT a correct laboratory test finding for polycythemia vera.

   A. CBC in all mature cell forms, i.e., erythrocytes, leukocytes, and platelets
   B. uric acid and decreased Hct
   C. bone marrow in mature cell forms and increased bilirubin (indirect) in unconjugated fraction
   D. liver enzymes with possible hematuria and melena

27. Regarding effective treatment of polycythemia vera,

   A. therapy must be individualized according to age, sex, medical status, clinical manifestations, and hematologic findings
   B. phlebotomy is an integral part of all therapeutic regimens and may be the only therapy. It is the treatment of choice for women of childbearing age and patients under age 40 since it is not mutagenic and symptoms of hypervolemia are eliminated
   C. myelosuppressive therapy may be indicated in patients with platelet counts greater than 1×10^6/uL, discomfort from visceral enlargement, thrombosis, symptoms from hypermetabolism or uncontrolled pruritis, and in elderly patients or those with cardiovascular disease who do not tolerate phlebotomy well
   D. all of the above

28. All of the following statements are correct regarding the drugs used for the treatment of polycythemia vera EXCEPT:

   A. Hyperuricemia can be managed with allopurinol orally 300 mg/day, and pruritis can be completely controlled by antihistamines
   B. Alkylating agents should be avoided since they are recognized to be leukemogenic
   C. Hydroxyurea, which acts by inhibiting the enzyme ribonucleoside diphosphate reductase, has been used successfully in younger patients when myelosuppressive therapy is indicated, and is not currently known to be leukemogenic. Patients are phlebotomized to a normal Hct (40-45%) and placed on hydroxyurea (10 to 15 mg/kg/day. The patient is monitored with a weekly blood count.

D. After phlebotomizing the patient to a normal Hct, ^{32}P 2.7 mCi/sq m BSA is given IV, the total dose not exceeding 5 mCi. This dose usually normalizes the platelet count and Hct within 4 to 8 weeks

29. To control Mr. Crockett,s condition, it would NOT be appropriate for a nurse to   29.____

   A. monitor for signs and symptoms of bleeding complications, force fluids, and record I and O
   B. prevent development of DVT and monitor for signs and symptoms of CHF
   C. provide care for phlebotomy
   D. administer cyclophosphamide as ordered for peptic ulcer

30. During the discharge planning conference, the nurse would provide Mr. Crockett with teaching and discharge planning concerning all of the following EXCEPT   30.____

   A. decrease in activity tolerance and the need to space activity with periods of rest
   B. high fluid intake and avoidance of food rich in vitamin C to avoid counteracting the therapeutic effects of phlebotomy
   C. recognition and reporting of bleeding
   D. need to avoid persons with infections, especially in leukopenic patients

---

KEY (CORRECT ANSWERS)

1.	C	16.	B
2.	D	17.	C
3.	D	18.	D
4.	D	19.	A
5.	C	20.	D
6.	B	21.	D
7.	C	22.	D
8.	D	23.	C
9.	C	24.	C
10.	A	25.	C
11.	A	26.	B
12.	D	27.	D
13.	B	28.	A
14.	A	29.	D
15.	D	30.	B

TEST 3

DIRECTIONS: Each question or Incomplete statement is followed by several suggested answers or completions. Select the one that BEST answers the question or completes the statement. *PRINT THE LETTER OF THE CORRECT ANSWER IN THE SPACE AT THE RIGHT.*

Questions 1-6.

DIRECTIONS: Questions 1 through 6 are to be answered on the basis of the following information.

48-year-old Gina Davis is brought to the hospital by her husband after having considerable nosebleeding and also noticing some bleeding under her skin.

1. After being examined by the physician, Mrs. Davis is diagnosed with idiopathic thrombocytopenic purpura (ITP), whose features include all of the following EXCEPT: 1.____

   A. The spleen is the site for destruction of platelets and is remarkably enlarged
   B. In children, it is usually a self-limited disorder that follows a viral infection
   C. In most adults, it is a chronic disorder with no apparent predisposing cause
   D. Increased destruction of platelets with resultant platelet count of less than 100,000/?/liter; characterized by petechiae and ecchymosis of the skin

2. While assessing Mrs. Davis, the nurse does NOT expect to notice 2.____

   A. petechiae: spider-web appearance of bleeding under skin due to small size of platelets
   B. pain wherever vaso-occlusive crisis occurs
   C. blood in any body secretions and bleeding from mucous membranes
   D. ecchymosis and nosebleeding

3. A CORRECT diagnostic test finding for ITP is 3.____

   A. decreased circulatory T_4 lymphocyte cells
   B. elevated serum globulins
   C. decreased platelet count and anemia
   D. elevated fibrin split products

4. All of the following would be appropriate nursing interventions to control Mrs. Davis, condition EXCEPT: 4.____

   A. To control bleeding, administer platelet transfusions as ordered and apply pressure to bleeding sites as needed
   B. Position bleeding part below heart level if possible
   C. Prevent bruising
   D. Provide support to patient and be sensitive to change in body image

5. Which of the following is NOT an appropriate nursing intervention for a patient of idiopathic thrombocytopenic purpura? 5.____

A. Measure normal circumference of extremities for baseline
B. Administer medications orally, rectally, or IV, rather than IM; if administering immunizations, give subcu-taneously (SC) and hold pressure on site for 5 minutes
C. Administer analgesics as ordered, aspirin being the most preferred
D. Provide care for the patient with a splenectomy

6. The nurse providing Mrs. Davis with teaching and discharge planning concerning prevention of trauma will NOT advise her to

   A. sew pads in knees and elbows of clothing
   B. keep weight to low normal to decrease extra stress on joints
   C. use stool softeners to prevent constipation
   D. avoid contact sports and suggest swimming, biking, golf, and pool

Questions 7-16.

DIRECTIONS: Questions 7 through 16 are to be answered on the basis of the following information.

48-year-old Scott Williams is brought to the emergency room by his wife after suffering headache, spinal cord compression, and, the most disturbing of all for Mr. Williams, bone pain increasing with activity.

7. After being carefully examined by the physician, Mr. Williams is diagnosed with multiple myeloma, which is BEST described as a progressive neoplastic disease characterized by

   A. marrow plasma cell tumors
   B. overproduction of intact monoclonal immunoglobulins IgG, IgA, IgD, or IgE and increased susceptibility to bacterial infections
   C. overproduction of Bence Jones Protein, and often associated with multiple osteolytic lesions, hyper-calcemia, anemia, renal damage, and increased susceptibility to bacterial infections
   D. all of the above

8. Multiple myeloma USUALLY occurs after age _____ and affects men _____ as often as women.

   A. 60; twice
   B. 50; half
   C. 40; twice
   D. 30; equally

9. Which of the following is an INCORRECT physiological finding about multiple myeloma?

   A. The pelvis, spine, ribs, skull, and lower extremities are most frequently involved.
   B. Skeletal x-rays may show diffuse osteoporosis or discrete osteolytic lesions due to replacement by expanding plasma cell tumors or a factor secreted by malignant plasma cells.
   C. Plasma cell tumors produce IgG in about 55% of myeloma patients and IgA in about 20%; 40% of these IgG and IgA patients also have Bence Jones Proteinuria.
   D. IgD myeloma is found in about 1% of cases with characteristic heavy Bence Jones proteinuria; only a few cases of IgE myeloma have been reported.

10. The nurse, while assessing Scott, may expect to notice all of the following EXCEPT 10.____

   A. pathologic fractures
   B. skeletal deformities of tibia, sternum, and ribs
   C. loss of height due to spinal column shortening
   D. osteoporosis

11. Of the following, the one that will NOT be an expected assessment finding while assessing a patient of multiple myeloma is 11.____

   A. renal calculi and hypocalcemia
   B. anemia, hemorrhagic tendencies, and increased susceptibility to infection
   C. renal dysfunction secondary to obstruction of convoluted tubules by coagulated protein particles
   D. neurologic dysfunction, i.e., spinal cord compression and paraplegia

12. An INCORRECT laboratory test finding for multiple myeloma is 12.____

   A. radiologic: diffuse bone lesions, widespread demineralization, osteoporosis, and osteolytic lesions of skull
   B. bone marrow: many immature plasma cells and depletion of other cell types
   C. Bence Jones protein positive and serum globulins depressed
   D. CBC: reduced Hgb, WBC, and platelet counts

13. APPROPRIATE therapy for a patient of multiple myeloma may include 13.____

   A. drug therapy
   B. radiation therapy to reduce tumor mass
   C. transfusion therapy
   D. all of the above

14. Effective drug therapy for multiple myeloma includes all of the following EXCEPT 14.____

   A. analgesics for bone pain
   B. chemotherapy by melphalan and cyclophosphamide to reduce tumor mass
   C. antibiotics for infection prophylaxis
   D. corticosteroids and mithramycin for severe hyper-calcemia

15. The one of the following that would NOT be considered appropriate nursing intervention to control Scott,s condition is: 15.____

   A. Provide comfort measures to help alleviate bone pain; encourage ambulation to slow demineralization process
   B. Encourage 6000-7000 cc/day of fluids to counteract calcium overload and to prevent protein from precipitating in the renal tubules
   C. Promote safety, as patient is prone to pathologic and other fractures; provide nursing care for bleeding tendencies and susceptibility to infection
   D. Provide a supportive atmosphere to enhance communication and reduce anxiety

16. The nurse would provide Scott teaching and discharge planning concerning 16.____

   A. crucial importance of long-term hydration to prevent urolithiasis and renal obstruction
   B. safety measures vital to decrease the risk of injury

C. avoidance of crowds or sources of infection due to leukopenia
D. all of the above

Questions 17-22.

DIRECTIONS: Questions 17 through 22 are to be answered on the basis of the following information.

34-year-old Fred Krueger is brought to the hospital by his wife after having weakness, difficulty breathing, and fever. Fred also complains of abdominal and bone pain.

17. After being carefully examined by the physician, Fred is diagnosed with acute nonlymphoblastic leukemia (ANLL), also known as acute myelocytic, myelogenous, myeloblastic, and myelomonoblastic, which is explained by all of the following EXCEPT:

    A. Accumulation of leukemic cells in the bone marrow replacing normal hematopoietic cells and spreading to the liver, spleen, lymph nodes, CNS, kidneys, and gonads. Since the cells are blood-borne, they can accumulate in and affect any organ or site.
    B. The accumulation of leukemic cells can always be identified with specific types of acute leukemia, e.g., acute myeloblastic leukemia is always recognized as localized collections in skin of or around the head and neck.
    C. Leukemic infiltration appears as sheets of undifferen-tiated round cells with usually minimal disruption of organ function except for the CNS and bone marrow.
    D. An uncontrolled proliferation of white blood cell precursors that fail to mature.

17.____

18. ANLL

    A. occurs in males and females of all ages
    B. is the more common type of acute leukemia among adults
    C. is the form usually associated with irradiation as a causative agent and occurring as a second malignancy following cancer chemotherapy
    D. all of the above

18.____

19. While assessing Fred, the nurse may expect to notice all of the following EXCEPT

    A. anemia, dyspnea, and pallor
    B. bleeding, petechiae, spontaneous bleeding, and ecchymoses
    C. infection due to excessive white blood cell production, fever, and malaise
    D. enlarged lymph nodes, spleen, and liver

19.____

20. Which of the following is NOT a correct laboratory finding used for the diagnosis of ANLL?

    A. Some degree of anemia and thrombocytopenia
    B. Total white blood cell count decreased, normal, or increased; leukemic blast cells in the blood smear unless the white blood cell count is markedly decreased
    C. Although the diagnosis can usually be made from the blood smear, a bone marrow examination should always be done for confirmation
    D. Touch preparations for cytology is the only way to perform biopsy specimen examination

20.____

21. All of the following are correct concerning the treatment of ANLL EXCEPT:

    A. The first goal of treatment is to achieve complete remission, which is associated with resolution of abnormal clinical features, return to normal blood counts, and hematopoiesis in the bone marrow with less than 5% blast cells
    B. Biologically, remission is associated with disappearance of the leukemic clone and restoration of normal polyclonal hematopoietic proliferation
    C. Supportive care requires blood bank, pharmacy, lab, and nursing services
    D. None of the above

22. An APPROPRIATE nursing intervention for a patient of ANLL would be to provide

    A. care for the patient receiving chemotherapy
    B. care for the patient receiving radiation therapy
    C. support for the patient and family since needs will change as treatment progresses
    D. all of the above

Questions 23-30.

DIRECTIONS: Questions 23 through 30 are to be answered on the basis of the following information.

36 year-old Rick Nelson comes to the hospital because of prolonged bleeding from a minor cut he got in his hand while preparing a fruit salad at home. Mr. Nelson also complains of painful knee and elbow joints with limited mobility.

23. After being examined by the physician, Mr. Nelson is diagnosed with hemophilia. Which of the following statements does NOT correctly explain hemophilia?

    A. A group of bleeding disorders when there is a deficit of one of several factors in the clotting mechanism. It is a sex-linked, inherited disorder whose classic form affects males only.
    B. If the individual has less than 40-50% of factor VIII or IX, there is an impairment of clotting and the clot is jelly-like.
    C. Only the intrinsic system is involved. Platelets are not affected, but fibrin clot does not always form. Bleeding from minor cuts may be stopped by platelets.
    D. It can be divided into three types: Hemophilia A, characterized by factor VIII deficiency, Hemophilia B, characterized by factor IX deficiency, and Hemophilia C, characterized by factor XI deficiency.

24. While assessing Mr. Nelson, the nurse may notice all of the following EXCEPT

    A. bruising, hematomas, and petechiae
    B. peripheral neuropathies due to bleeding near peripheral nerves including pain, paresthesias, and muscle atrophy
    C. repeated bleeding into a joint, resulting in a swollen and painful joint with limited mobility
    D. hemarthrosis resulting in contractures and possible degeneration of joint. Knees, elbows, ankles, and wrists are most often affected.

25. Assessment findings concerning prolonged bleeding after minor injury in children will NOT include

    A. at birth, after cutting of cord
    B. following the loss of baby teeth
    C. following intravenous immunizations
    D. increased bruising as a child learns to crawl and walk

26. Which of the following is NOT considered a correct diagnostic test finding of hemophilia?

    A. Normal platelet count
    B. Prolonged coagulation time
    C. Anemia
    D. Decreased PTT

27. All of the following would be appropriate nursing interventions to control an acute bleeding episode EXCEPT

    A. applying ice compresses for vasoconstriction
    B. immobilizing the area to prevent clots from being dislodged
    C. maintaining a calm environment to decrease blood pressure
    D. avoiding sutures, cauterization, and aspirin, as they exacerbate bleeding

28. A nurse providing care for hemarthrosis should NOT

    A. immobilize the joint and elevate it in a slightly flexed position. Avoid excessive handling of joint.
    B. administer analgesics as ordered. Pain relief will minimize increase in pulse rate and blood loss.
    C. instruct the patient to avoid weight bearing for 24 hours after bleeding episode if bleeding is in lower extremities
    D. provide active or passive ROM exercises after bleeding has been controlled (48 hours), as long as the exercises do not cause pain or irritate the trauma site

29. All of the following are appropriate procedures and information used to administer cryoprecipitate (frozen factor VIII) EXCEPT

    A. thaw slowly
    B. gently rotate the bottle, as shaking deteriorates antihemophilic factor
    C. infuse immediately when thawed
    D. factor VIII deteriorates at 60° C

30. The nurse providing teaching and discharge planning information to Mr. Nelson will NOT

    A. to avoid trauma, instruct him not to practice sports like biking, swimming, golf, or pool
    B. tell him to use soft toothettes instead of bristle toothbrushes
    C. discuss that when the mother is a carrier, there is a 50% chance with each pregnancy for her sons to have hemophilia and a 50% chance with each pregnancy for her daughters to be carriers
    D. discuss that when the father has hemophilia and the mother is normal, there is no chance for their children to have the disease, but all their daughters will be carriers

KEY (CORRECT ANSWERS)

1.	A	16.	D
2.	B	17.	B
3.	C	18.	D
4.	B	19.	C
5.	C	20.	D
6.	C	21.	D
7.	D	22.	D
8.	C	23.	B
9.	A	24.	A
10.	B	25.	C
11.	A	26.	D
12.	C	27.	C
13.	D	28.	C
14.	C	29.	D
15.	B	30.	A

EXAMINATION SECTION
TEST 1

DIRECTIONS: Each question or incomplete statement is followed by several suggested answers or completions. Select the one that BEST answers the question or completes the statement. *PRINT THE LETTER OF THE CORRECT ANSWER IN THE SPACE AT THE RIGHT*

Questions 1-10.

DIRECTIONS: Questions 1 through 10 are to be answered on the basis of the following information.

58-year-old Julie Fields is brought to the hospital by her husband after having enlarged nodes in the lower cervical region. Mrs. Fields also has fever and complains of night sweats.

1. After being examined by the physician, Mrs. Fields is diagnosed with Hodgkin's lymphoma, which may BEST be described as a(n) _____ disease with _____ that may be present in localized or disseminated form.
    A. chronic; lymphatic proliferation
    B. acute; reticular proliferation
    C. chronic; lymphoreticular proliferation of unknown cause
    D. acute; lymphoreticular proliferation of various causes

1._____

2. Which of the following is NOT a true fact about the incidence of Hodgkin's lymphoma?
    A. Annually in the United States, 5000 to 6000 new cases are diagnosed.
    B. The male: female ratio is 1.4:1.
    C. Rare before age 10, a binodal age distribution exists with one peak at ages 15 to 34 and another after age 54.
    D. Epidemiologic studies find considerable evidence of horizontal spread.

2._____

3. A CORRECT etiology finding about Hodgkin's lymphoma is:
    A. It resembles a low-grade graft-versus-host reaction
    B. Recent. evidence of tumor-associated antigens in Hodgkin's tissue is consistent with interpretation given in para A
    C. A number of infectious agents, including viruses, are postulated as causes
    D. All of the above

3._____

4. The one of the following that is NOT one of the four histopathologic classifications of Hodgkin's lymphoma is:
    A. Lymphocyte predominance - few Reed-Sternberg cells and many lymphocytes
    B. Mixed cellularity - an increased number of Reed-Sternberg cells with a mixed infiltrate
    C. Nodular sclerosis - generally, a moderate number of Reed-Sternberg cells with a mixed infiltrate except that dense fibrous tissue, which shows characteristic birefringence with polarized light, surrounds nodules of Hodgkin's tissue
    D. Lymphocyte depletion - few lymphocytes, numerous Reed-Sternberg cells, and extensive fibrosis or abnormal reticulum cell infiltrate

4._____

5. While assessing Mrs. Fields, the nurse may expect to notice all of the following EXCEPT
    A. pruritis and petechiae
    B. recurrent, intermittent fever
    C. weight loss, malaise, and lethargy
    D. enlarged nodes in the lower cervical region; nodes are nontender, firm, and moveable

5._____

6. The diagnosis of Hodgkin's lymphoma depends upon the identification of
   A. small multinucleated lymphatic cells in lymph node tissue
   B. large multinucleated reticulum cells, also named Reed-Sternberg cells, in lymph node tissue or other sites
   C. large multinucleated lymphoreticular cells in lymph nodes
   D. all of the above

7. Which of the following will NOT be part of Mrs. Fields' medical management?
   A. Lymphangiogram: determines the involvement of all the lymph nodes, is reliable in 90% of patients, and is helpful in determining radiation fields
   B. Laparotomy and splenectomy
   C. Lymph node biopsy to identify the presence of Reed-Sternberg cells and for hematologic classification
   D. Radiation: used alone for localized disease

8. Hodgkin's lymphoma staging via laparotomy and biopsy shows all of the following except Stage
   A. I: single lymph node involved, usually in neck, 90% to 98% survival
   B. II: involvement of 6 or more lymph nodes on same side of diaphragm, 70-80% survival
   C. III: involvement of lymph nodes on both sides of diaphragm, 50% survival
   D. IV: metastasis to other organs

9. Chemotherapy is used in conjunction with radiation therapy for advanced disease. The drug combination of choice for Hodgkin's lymphoma is
   A. adriamycin, bleomycin, procarbazine, and prednisone (ABPP)
   B. mechlorethamine vincristine (oncovin), adriamycin, and dacarbazine (MOAD)
   C. nitrosoureas, streptozocin, cis-platinum, and epipodophyllotoxin (VP-16)
   D. mechlorethamine, vincristine (oncovin), procarbazine, and prednisone (MOPP)

10. An IMPORTANT nursing intervention for Hodgkin's lymphoma would be to
    A. provide care for a patient receiving radiation therapy
    B. administer chemotherapy as ordered and monitor/ alleviate the side effects
    C. protect patients from infection, especially if splenectomy is performed
    D. all of the above

Questions 11-18.

DIRECTIONS: Questions 11 through 18 are to be answered on the basis of the following information.
36-year-old Nancy Drew is brought to the hospital by her husband after having marked respiratory distress. Mrs. Drew also has a family history of allergies.

11. After being examined, Mrs. Drew is diagnosed with bronchial asthma, which may be accurately described by all of the following EXCEPT:
    A. A reversible obstructive lung disorder characterized by increased responsiveness of the airways
    B. Often caused by an allergic reaction to an environmental allergen, and always Seasonal
    C. Immunologic/allergic reaction results in histamine release, which produces three main airway responses, i.e., edema of mucous membranes and spasm of the smooth muscle of bronchi and bronchioles and accumulation of tenacious secretions
    D. Status asthmaticus occurs when there is little response to treatment and symptoms persist

12. The one of the following pathophysiological findings that is NOT true about bronchial asthma is:
    A. Airway obstruction causes hypoventilation in some lung areas, and continued blood flow to these areas leads to a ventilation/perfusion imbalance resulting in hypoxemia. Arterial hypoxemia is almost always present in attacks severe enough to require medical attention.
    B. Hyperventilation occurs early in the attack and results in a decrease in PaCO$_2$. As the attack progresses, the patient's capacity to compensate by hyperventilation of unobstructed areas of the lung is further impaired by more extensive airways narrowing and muscular fatigue. Arterial hypoxemia worsens and PaCO$_2$ begins to rise, leading respiratory acidosis. At this point, the patient is said to be in respiratory failure, stage IV of an acute attack.
    C. An imbalance between 13-adrenergic and cholinergic control of airways diameter has been proposed, one of the facts being a decreased cholinergic responsiveness because most asthmatics respond excessively with bronchoconstriction after inhalation of cholinergic agents and because atropine and its derivatives can often partially block irritant-induced bronchocon-striction.
    D. The observed abnormalities in adrenergic and cholinergic functions in asthma appear to be controlled by the cyclic 3',5' - adenosine monophosphate (Camp) cyclic 3',5' - guanosine monophosphate (cGMP) systems within various tissues, e.g., mast cells, smooth muscle, and mucus-secreting cells

13. While assessing Mrs. Drew, the nurse may expect to notice all of the following EXCEPT
    A. family history of infections by gram-negative aerobic cocci
    B. patient history of eczema
    C. shortness of breath, expiratory wheeze, prolonged expiratory phase, air trapping (barrel chest if chronic)
    D. use of accessory muscles, irritability (from hypoxia), diaphoresis, change in sensorium if severe attack

14. Which of the following is NOT true regarding laboratory finding in asthma?
    A. Eosinophilia is commonly present, regardless of whether allergic factors can be shown to have an etiologic role. Blood eosinophilia greater than 250 to 400 cells/μL is the rule.
    B. Determination of arterial blood gases and pH is essential to the adequate evaluation of a patient with asthma of sufficient severity to warrant hospitalization.
    C. Chest x-ray findings varying from normal to hypo-inflation. Lung markings are increased, particularly in chronic disease. The expiratory x-rays are especially important in the case of non-opaque foreign bodies.
    D. Pulmonary function tests are valuable in differential diagnosis, and also in known asthmatics to assess the degree of airway obstruction and disturbance in gas exchange, to measure the airways' response to inhaled allergens and chemicals, to quantify the response to drugs, and for long-term follow-up

15. The INCORRECT statement about diagnostic tests for asthma is
    A. Static lung volumes and capacities reveal various combinations of abnormalities. Of the tests most often used clinically, total lung capacity (TLC), functional residual capacity (FRC), and residual volume (RV) are usually increased. Vital capacity (VC) may be normal or increased.
    B. The confirmation of extrinsic allergic factors is best accomplished by an allergy evaluation that includes allergy skin testing with extracts to detect IgE antibody to inhalants and other allergens suggested by the patient's history.

C. Specific IgE antibody to inhalants may also be detected by a radioallergosorbent test (RAST) on the patient's serum, but this test is expensive, subject to laboratory error, and offers little advantage over properly done and interpreted skin tests.
D. Inhalational bronchial challenge testing has been used (1) with allergens to establish the clinical significance of positive skin tests, (2) with methacoline or histamine to assess the degree of airway hyperactivity in known asthmatics, or (3) to aid in diagnosing asthma when the symptoms are atypical.

16. When performing a physical examination of a patient with asthma, the one of the following that does NOT apply is:
    A. You should search for heart failure and signs of chronic hypoxemia, such as clubbing of the fingers
    B. Nasal polyposis should suggest aspirin intolerance
    C. A unilateral wheezing should provoke a search for obstruction by a foreign body, vascular malformation, aneurysm, or tumor
    D. In tracheal obstruction, an inspiratory wheeze is present over the lower airway

17. All of the following would be appropriate nursing interventions to control Mrs. Drew's condition EXCEPT:
    A. administering oxygen as ordered and placing patient in low-Fowler's position
    B. providing humidification/hydration to loosen secretions
    C. providing chest percussion and postural drainage when bronchodilation improves
    D. monitoring for respiratory distress

18. Mrs. Drew has recovered and is ready to be discharged.
    The nurse will provide her with teaching and discharge planning concerning all of the following EXCEPT
    A. stay indoors during grass cutting or when pollen count is high
    B. avoid natural fibers like wool and feathers; avoid rugs, stuffed animals, and draperies or curtains
    C. importance of moderate exercises with contraindication of swimming
    D. purpose of breathing exercises to increase the end expiratory pressure of each respiration

Questions 19-26.

DIRECTIONS: Questions 19 through 26 are to be answered on the basis of the following information.
48-year-old Moe Link is admitted into the hospital because of mild chest pain. He is 5 feet, 8 inches tall and weighs 198 pounds. A myocardial infarction is diagnosed.

19. Oxygen by nasal cannula is prescribed for Mr. Link. Safety precautions would be used by the nurse in the room because oxygen
    A. has unstable properties
    B. may convert to an alternate form
    C. is flammable
    D. supports combustion

20. Isoenzyme laboratory studies are ordered.
    The isoenzyme test that is the MOST reliable early indicator of myocardial insult is
    A. AST　　　　　B. SGPT　　　　　C. CPK　　　　　D. LDH

21. An electrocardiogram is ordered. 21.____
    An early finding in the lead over the infarcted area would be
    A. absence of T waves
    B. flattened P waves
    C. elevated ST segments
    D. disappearance of Q waves

22. The physician orders 8 mg. of morphine sulfate to be given by injection. The vial on hand 22.____
    is labeled 1 ml =10 mg.
    The nurse should administer _____ minims.
    A. 8
    B. 12
    C. 16
    D. 20

23. Mr. Link wants to know why he is given the injection of morphine. 23.____
    The nurse explains to him that it
    A. decreases anxiety and restlessness
    B. contracts coronary b000d vessels
    C. relieves pain and prevents shock
    D. helps prevent fibrillation of heart

24. Mr. Link, who was admitted three days earlier, is complaining to the nurse about 24.____
    numerous aspects of his hospital stay.
    The BEST initial nursing response would be to
    A. try to explain the purpose of different hospital routines
    B. refocus the conversation on his anger, fears, and frustrations about his condition
    C. allow him to express his feelings and then promptly leave to permit him to regain his composure
    D. explain how his upset condition dangerously interferes with his need for rest

25. Several days after admission, Mr. Link develops pyrexia. 25.____
    One of the adaptations related to the pyrexia that the nurse would monitor him for would be
    A. depressed blood pressure
    B. back pain
    C. increased pulse rate
    D. dyspnea

26. Mr. Link asks the nurse about his chances of having another heart attack if he watches 26.____
    his diet and stress levels carefully.
    The MOST appropriate initial response by the nurse would be to
    A. avoid giving him direct information and help him explore his feelings
    B. suggest to him that he discuss his feelings of vulnerability with his physician
    C. recognize that he is frightened and suggest that he talk with the psychologic nurse
    D. tell him that he certainly needs to be careful in these areas

Questions 27-30.
DIRECTIONS: Questions 27 through 30 are to be answered on the basis of the following information.
56-year-old Holly Parton is having a workup for pernicious anemia.

27. A Schilling test is ordered for Mrs. Parton. 27.____
    The nurse should know that the PRIMARY purpose of the Schilling test is to determine the patient's ability to _____ vitamin B_{12}.
    A. produce
    B. metabolize
    C. store
    D. absorb

28. Pernicious anemia is confirmed, and the physician orders 0.4 mg of cyanocobalamin IM. The available vial of the drug is labeled 1 ml = 100 mcg. The nurse should administer _____ ml.
    A. 1   B. 2   C. 3   D. 4

29. When you tell Mrs. Parton the therapeutic regimen about vitamin B12, the nurse should tell her that
    A. intramuscular injections are required weekly for control
    B. oral supplements taken daily will control her symptoms
    C. intramuscular injections once a month will control the symptoms
    D. monthly Z-track injections will provide the required control

30. Mrs. Parton understands the instructions regarding the vitamin B_{12} injections when the nurse states that she must take it
    A. during exacerbations of anemia
    B. when she feels hypertensed
    C. until her symptoms are controlled
    D. for the rest of her life

KEY (CORRECT ANSWERS)

1. C	11. B	21. C
2. D	12. C	22. B
3. D	13. A	23. C
4. B	14. C	24. B
5. A	15. A	25. C
6. B	16. D	26. A
7. C	17. A	27. D
8. B	18. C	28. D
9. D	19. D	29. C
10. D	20. C	30. D

TEST 2

DIRECTIONS: Each question or incomplete statement is followed by several suggested answers or completions. Select the one that BEST answers the question or completes the statement. *PRINT THE LETTER OF THE CORRECT ANSWER IN THE SPACE AT THE RIGHT*

Questions 1-12.

DIRECTIONS: Questions 1 through 12 are to be answered on the basis of the following information.

46-year-old Tanya Hardin is brought to the hospital by her husband after having enlarged lymph nodes which are rubbery and discrete. Mrs. Hardin also complains of weight loss and fever with night sweats.

1. After being examined by the physician, Mrs. Hardin is diagnosed with Non-Hodgkin's lymphoma, which may BEST be described as
    A. a heterogeneous group of diseases consisting of neo-plastic proliferation of lymphoid cells that usually disseminate throughout the body
    B. a heterogeneous group of diseases, which includes a wide range of disease entities, e.g., lymphosarcoma, reticulum cell sarcoma, and Burkitt's lymphoma
    C. primary sites include gastrointestinal tract, ovaries, testes, bones, CNS, liver, breast, and subcutaneous tissues
    D. all of the above

1._____

2. Which of the following age groups is MOST affected by Non-Hodgkin's lymphoma?
    A. Women age 40 and over
    B. Men age 40 and over
    C. Both men and women age 40 and over
    D. All age groups

2._____

3. Close association of Type _____ with some adult leukemias and lymphomas comprised of peripheral T cells has been demonstrated in recent years.
    A. adenovirus   B. rhinovirus   C. retrovirus   D. reovirus

3._____

4. Of the following human T-cell leukemia-lymphoma viruses (HTLV), the one that has been isolated from several patients and appears to be endemic to Japan, the Caribbean, South America, and certain regions of the United States is HTLV-
    A. I   B. II   C. III   D. IV

4._____

5. The Rappaport classification for the histopathology of NHL is based on the degree of differentiation of the tumor, and on the presence or absence of nodules. All classes are divided into nodular or diffuse.
    The class that occurs ONLY in a diffuse pattern is malignant lymphoma,
    A. histiocytic
    B. undifferentiated Burkitt's type or non-Burkitt's pleomorphic type
    C. lymphocytic
    D. mixed lymphocytic-histiocytic

5._____

123

6. The Lukes and Collins classification, which is based upon the cell of origin, divides NHL into
    A. T cell (thymus-derived) types that include immunoblastic sarcoma and convoluted cell lymphoma, similar to lymphoblastic lymphoma. Occurs in about 15% of all cases.
    B. cell (bone marrow-derived) types that include well-differentiated lymphocytic, plasmacytic, follicular center cell lymphomas, and a B-cell immunoblastic sarcoma. Occurs in about 75% of all cases.
    C. *true* histiocytic or monocytic origin type. Occurs in about 5% of all cases.
    D. all of the above

7. The new International Panel Working Formulation separates NHL into all of the following categories EXCEPT _____, described as _____ types.
    A. *low grade or favorable-prognosis lymphomas*; diffuse, well-differentiated; nodular, poorly differentiated lymphocytic; and nodular-mixed
    B. *intermediate-grade or prognosis lymphomas*; nodular histiocytic; diffuse, poorly differentiated, lymphocytic; and diffuse-mixed
    C. *high grade or unfavorable-prognosis lymphomas*; diffuse histiocytic lymphoma; diffuse undifferentiated; and lymphoblastic T cell lymphoma
    D. *highest grade or no prognosis lymphomas*; non-composite lymphomas, false histiocytic, other, and unclassifiable

8. While assessing Mrs. Hardin, the nurse should NOT expect to notice
    A. asymptomatic adenopathy involving cervical or inguinal regions, or both
    B. anemia, which is initially present in about 33% of patients and eventually develops in most. It may be due to bleeding from GI involvement or low platelet levels, hemolysis due to hypersplenism or Coombs-positive hemolytic anemia, bone marrow infiltration by lymphoma, or marrow suppression by drugs or irradiation
    C. a leukemic phase, which develops in 40-60% of lymphocytic lymphomas and 20% of histiocytic lymphomas
    D. hypogammaglobulinemia due to progressive decrease in immunoglobulin production, which occurs in 15% of patients and may predispose to serious bacterial infection

9. All of the following are correct about the treatment of early NHL disease (stages I and II) EXCEPT:
    A. With low and intermediate-grade lymphomas, patients rarely present with localized disease, but, when they do, regional radiotherapy offers long-term control and sometimes cure
    B. Those with high-grade lymphomas are generally treated with combination chemotherapy with or without regional radiotherapy
    C. Cure rates vary from 40 to 60%
    D. None of the above

10. In the treatment of advanced disease (stages III and IV),
    A. a watch and wait approach, treatment with a single alkylating agent, or 2- and 3-drug programs may be used
    B. interferon as well as other biologic response modifiers have resulted in some encouraging remissions
    C. while survival may be prolonged, relapse eventually occurs and cure rates are generally less than 20 to 25%
    D. all of the above

11. In patients with intermediate-grade lymphomas, combinations of certain drugs with or without adriamycin result in complete regression of disease in 50 to 70% of patients. In these cases, a pattern of continuous late relapse usually occurs, however, and only 20 to 30% are cured.
    These drugs are _____, vincristine, and _____.
    A. procarbazine; prednisone
    B. cyclophosphamide; prednisone
    C. mechlorethamine; procarbazine
    D. nitrosoureas; streptozocin

11._____

12. Patients having lymphomas with unfavorable-prognosis histology usually have rapid tumor growth (high grade), but modern intensive combination chemotherapy programs have dramatically reversed the previously poor cure rate of less than 10%.
    Use of a _____ drug program with acronyms has resulted in complete remission rates of 50 to 70% with about 40 to 60% of all patients being cured.
    A. 4   B. 5   C. 6   D. all of the above

12._____

Questions 13-20.

DIRECTIONS: Questions 13 through 20 are to be answered on the basis of the following information.

56-year-old Jerry West visits the hospital after having a cough with sputum production, anorexia, and fatigue. Mr. West has also been a cigarette smoker since he was 20.

13. After being examined by the physician, Mr. West is diagnosed with emphysema. All of the following statements give correct information about the disease EXCEPT:
    A. Contraction of tracheal muscles with resultant loss of recoil occurs
    B. Enlargement and destruction of the alveolar, bronchial, and bronchiolar tissue with resultant loss of recoil, air trapping, thoracic overdistension, sputum accumulation, and loss of diaphragmatic muscle tone occur
    C. The changes given above in B. cause a state of carbon dioxide retention, hypoxia, and respiratory acidosis
    D. The disease is caused by cigarette smoking, infection, inhaled irritants, heredity, allergic factors, and aging

13._____

14. While assessing Mr. West, the nurse will NOT expect to notice
    A. weight loss and decreased rate and depth of breathing
    B. dyspnea, feeling of breathlessness, and sputum production
    C. flaring of the nostrils and use of accessory muscles of respiration
    D. decreased respiratory excursion, resonance to hyper-resonance, decreased breath sounds with prolonged expiration, and normal or decreased fremitus

14._____

15. A CORRECT diagnostic test finding for emphysema is PCO_2 _____ and PO_2 _____.
    A. elevated; normal
    B. normal; slightly decreased
    C. elevated; slightly increased
    D. elevated or normal; normal or slightly decreased

15._____

16. All of the following are accurate pathological findings of emphysema EXCEPT:
    A. Microscopic examination reveals departitioning of the lung due to loss of alveolar walls; large bullae may be present in advanced disease
    B. In severe emphysema, the lungs are large and pale and always fail to collapse when the thorax is opened
    C. Changes may be most marked in the center of the acinus, i.e., centrilobular emphysema or more diffusely scattered throughout the lobule, i.e., panacinar emphysema. In all forms, normal architecture is destroyed and loss of alveolar walls results in air sacs of various sizes.
    D. The abnormalities lead not only to a reduction in the area of alveolar membrane available for gas exchange, but also to the perfusion of nonventilated areas and to the ventilation of nonperfused parts of the lung, i.e., ventilation/perfusion (V/Q) abnormalities

17. CORRECT drug therapy in the treatment of emphysema includes the use of
    A. bronchodilators such as aminophylline, isoproterenol (isuprel), terbutaline (brethine), metaproterenol (alupent), theophylline, and isoetharine (bronkosol) to treat bronchospasm
    B. tetracycline and ampicillin to treat bacterial infections
    C. prednisone as a corticosteroid
    D. all of the above

18. All of the following would be appropriate nursing interventions to control Mr. West's condition EXCEPT
    A. assuring fluid intake of at least 5 liters a day
    B. facilitating removal of secretions by providing chest physical therapy, coughing, and deep breathing, and use of hand nebulizers
    C. improving ventilation by placing him in semi- or high-Fowler's position
    D. instructing him to use diaphragmatic muscle to breathe; employing pursed-lip breathing techniques

19. All of the following would be appropriate teaching and discharge planning provided by the nurse to Mr. West concerning prevention of recurrent infections EXCEPT;
    A. Avoid crowds and individuals with known infection
    B. Adhere to a high-protein, high-carbohydrate, and increased vitamin C diet
    C. Receive immunizations for influenza, pneumonia, and tuberculosis
    D. Report changes in characteristics and color of sputum immediately; report Worsening of symptoms like increased tightness of chest, fatigue, and increased dyspnea

20. Which of the following will NOT be a part of teaching and discharge planning provided by the nurse to Mr. West concerning environmental control and avoidance of inhaled irritants?
    A. Use home humidifier at 30-50% humidity
    B. Wear a scarf over nose and mouth in very hot weather to prevent bronchospasm
    C. Avoid smoking and others who smoke; avoid abrupt changes in temperature
    D. Use an air conditioner with a high-efficiency particulate air filter to remove particles from the air

Questions 21-25.

DIRECTIONS: Questions 21 through 25 are to be answered on the basis of the following information.

22-year-old David Quinn, a military recruit, visits the hospital after having a fever and enlarged, red tonsils.

21. After being examined by the physician, David is diagnosed with tonsillitis, which is a (n) _____, usually due to _____ infection.
    A. acute inflammation of the tonsils; streptococcal or, less commonly, fungal
    B. chronic inflammation of the tonsils; bacterial or, less commonly, viral
    C. acute inflammation of the palatine tonsils; streptococcal or, less commonly, viral
    D. chronic inflammation of the palatine tonsils; staphylococcal or, less commonly, streptococcal

21._____

22. _____% of tonsillitis is caused by group A beta-hemolytic streptococci.
    A. 10-15   B. 15-20   C. 20-25   D. 25-30

22._____

23. While assessing David, the nurse may expect to notice all of the following EXCEPT
    A. sore throat and pain, most marked on swallowing and often referred to the nostrils
    B. high fever, malaise, headache, and vomiting
    C. white patches of exudate on tonsillar pillars
    D. enlarged cervical lymph nodes

23._____

24. Penicillin G or V is the treatment of choice for streptococcal tonsillitis and should be continued for 10 days.
    The APPROPRIATE dosage would be _____ every _____ hours.
    A. 250 mg orally; 6   B. 325 mg IM; 8   C. 500 mg IV; 10   D. all of the above

24._____

25. When possible, the patient's throat should be recultured 5 to 6 days after treatment is over. Family members' throats should also be cultured initially so that carriers may be treated at the same time.
    Tonsillectomy should be considered if
    A. despite the above given precautions acute tonsillitis repeatedly develops after adequate treatment
    B. chronic tonsillitis and sore throat persist
    C. chronic tonsillitis and sore throat are relieved only briefly by antibiotic therapy
    D. all of the above

25._____

KEY (CORRECT ANSWERS)

1.	D		11.	B
2.	D		12.	D
3.	C		13.	A
4.	A		14.	A
5.	B		15.	D
6.	D		16.	B
7.	D		17.	D
8.	C		18.	A
9.	D		19.	C
10.	D		20.	B

21. C
22. A
23. A
24. A
25. D

EXAMINATION SECTION
TEST 1

DIRECTIONS: Each question or incomplete statement is followed by several suggested answers or completions. Select the one that BEST answers the question or completes the statement. *PRINT THE LETTER OF THE CORRECT ANSWER IN THE SPACE AT THE RIGHT.*

Questions 1-9.

DIRECTIONS: Questions 1 through 9 are to be answered on the basis of the following information.

Ms. Evelyn Hart, a 75-year-old widow, is admitted to a psychiatric hospital. Her son, who brings her, says that she has been confused and wandered away from home. Also, she has become increasingly careless about her appearance.

1. With a chronic brain syndrome such as Ms. Hart's, the personality changes are MOST often manifested as.   1.____

   A. an exaggeration of previous traits
   B. overt pleas for assistance
   C. suspicion and reticence
   D. marked resistance and negativism

2. During the early period following Ms. Hart's admission, the nursing procedure that would be BEST for her is   2.____

   A. carrying out activities in the same order each day
   B. insisting that she focus her conversation on present events
   C. providing a variety of novel experiences
   D. rotating staff assignments so that she will become acquainted with each member of the nursing staff

3. When Ms. Hart's son comes to visit her the day after admission, Ms. Hart refuses to talk to him. The son goes to the nurse and says, *My mother won't talk to me. Why is she acting like this? I had to do something with her. I couldn't keep her with us. Oh, what a mess!* Which of these responses by the nurse would be MOST appropriate initially?   3.____

   A. You feel guilty about having your mother here.
   B. Your mother is having a little difficulty adjusting to the hospital.
   C. This is a difficult situation for you and your mother.
   D. I'm sure you did the best you could under the circumstances.

4. Ms. Hart's son asks the nurse whether he should come to see his mother again on the following day in view of her reaction to his first visit.
Which of these responses would be BEST?   4.____

   A. Advising the son to wait until his mother gives some indication that she is ready to see him
   B. Suggesting that the son come back the next day since his continuing interest is important to his mother

C. Telling the son that his mother will not miss him if he doesn't visit because she will become attached to staff members
D. Informing the son that it is important for his mother to have visitors and suggesting that he ask one of her friends to visit her

5. The nurse finds Ms. Hart standing near the lavatory door. She has wet herself - as she does occasionally - because she does not allow herself sufficient time to reach the bathroom. Ms. Hart looks ashamed and turns her head away from the nurse.
Which of these responses by the nurse would be BEST?

   A. Asking, *Can you tell me why you wait so long, Ms. Hart?*
   B. Saying, *I know that this is upsetting to you, Ms. Hart. Come with me and I'll get a change of clothes for you*
   C. Asking, *Can you think of any way in which we can help you to manage your bathroom trips, Ms. Hart?*
   D. Sending Ms. Hart to her room to change her clothing

6. At about 3 P.M. one day, Ms. Hart comes to the nurse and says, *J haven't had a thing to eat all day.* The nurse knows that Ms. Hart did have lunch.
Which of these understandings by the nurse should be BASIC to a response?

   A. Confabulation is used by elderly patients as a means of relieving anxiety.
   B. Hunger is symbolic of a feeling of deprivation.
   C. Retrospective falsification is a mechanism commonly used by elderly persons who are unhappy.
   D. Loss of memory for recent events is characteristic of patients with senile dementia.

7. Ms. Hart is to be encouraged to increase her intake of protein.
The addition of which of these foods to 100 cc. of milk will provide the GREATEST amount of protein?

   A. 50 cc. light cream and 2 tablespoons corn syrup
   B. 30 grams powdered skim milk and 1 egg
   C. 1 small scoop (90 grams) vanilla ice cream and 1 tablespoon chocolate syrup
   D. 2 egg yolks and 1 tablespoon sugar

8. One day when another patient, Mr. Simon, is about to go to the canteen, Ms. Hart says to him, *Bring me a candy bar.* Mr. Simon replies, *Okay, give me the twenty-five cents for it.* Ms. Hart struggles with the idea, taking out a quarter and holding it but not giving it to Mr. Simon. Mr. Simon goes off impatiently, and Ms. Hart looks forlorn.
Which of these responses by the nurse would probably be MOST useful to Ms. Hart?

   A. *Ms. Hart, when we get things from the canteen, we have to pay for them. Do you want to buy candy?*
   B. *It was hard for you to decide whether or not to give Mr. Simon the money for the candy. Let's go to the canteen together.*
   C. *I know you are upset about Mr. Simon's going off, but he did have a right to ask you for the money for the candy.*
   D. *You feel you annoyed Mr. Simon. Would you like to talk about it?*

9. Ms. Hart tells stories over and over about her childhood. One day she keeps talking about holidays and how she used to make cookies for visiting children.
Which of the responses by the nurse would be BEST?

   A. That must have been a lot of fun, Ms. Hart. Will you help us make popcorn balls for the unit party?
   B. I can understand that those things were important to you, Ms. Hart. Now we can talk about something that is going on in the unit.
   C. Things are different now, Ms. Hart. What does your family serve as party refreshments nowadays?
   D. Those were the good old days. Did you ever go on a hayride?

Questions 10-17.

DIRECTIONS: Questions 10 through 17 are to be answered on the basis of the following information.

Mr. David Tripp, 28 years old, is brought from his place of work to the emergency department of a local general hospital by the police. He had been threatening his supervisor, who had criticized his work. During the admission procedure, he says, *They're all in on the plot to lock me up so I can't protect the world from them.*

10. During the early period of Mr. Tripp's hospitalization, which of these plans of care would probably be BEST for him?

   A. Encourage him to enter into simple group activities.
   B. Establish a daily routine that will help him become oriented to this new environment.
   C. Plan to cope with his slowness in carrying out his daily schedule.
   D. Assign the same members of the nursing team to care for him each day.

11. Mr. Tripp is on chlorpromazine hydrochloride (Thorazine) 100 mg. t.i.d. and 200 mg. at h.s.
The CHIEF purpose of chlorpromazine for Mr. Tripp is to

   A. relieve his anxiety
   B. control his aggression
   C. decrease his psychotic symptoms
   D. alleviate his depression

12. Mr. Tripp is walking into the dayroom when a male patient runs toward him screaming, *Let me out! Let me out!* A nurse's aide is following the screaming patient and is talking soothingly to him. Mr. Tripp seems panic-stricken and turns to flee.
Which of these initial responses to Mr. Tripp by the nurse would be BEST?

   A. Don't go, Mr. Tripp. That patient won't hurt you. He is frightened.
   B. It is upsetting to hear someone scream. The aide will help that patient. I will stay with you for a while, Mr. Tripp.
   C. Don't be upset, Mr. Tripp. That patient is sicker than you are. It's all right for you to go to your room if you like.
   D. This is nothing to be disturbed about, Mr. Tripp. It is part of that patient's illness.

13. One afternoon, Mr. Tripp is sitting in a small lounge watching a TV news program. During 13.____
a biographical sketch of a criminal, Mr. Tripp begins to shout frantically, No, I am not one!
You've no right to say that! Mr. Tripp's response to the program is MOST clearly an example of

    A. an idea of reference   B. an obsession
    C. confabulation   D. negativism

14. Mr. Tripp seems to value his regular sessions with the nurse, but on one occasion he 14.____
becomes agitated and suddenly gets up and starts to mumble and pace back and forth.
Which of these actions by the nurse would be BEST when Mr. Tripp does this?

    A. Sit quietly, while remaining attentive to him.
    B. Join him and pace with him.
    C. Leave the room until he calms down.
    D. Get a male nurse's aide to come and stand by and observe Mr. Tripp.

15. Mr. Tripp, who has read widely in the field of psychology, quotes fluently from various 15.____
authorities with whose works the nurse is only vaguely acquainted.
Which of these actions by the nurse in this situation would probably be BEST?

    A. Make an attempt to learn more about psychology in order to be able to converse with Mr. Tripp.
    B. Point out to Mr. Tripp that such theoretical knowledge is of little value unless it is applied in daily life.
    C. Listen attentively, in a relaxed manner, without attempting to compete with Mr. Tripp.
    D. Ask Mr. Tripp if he understands why he feels the need to give evidence of his knowledge of psychology.

16. Mr. Tripp is much improved and is to go home for a weekend. Since he is taking chlorpro- 16.____
mazine hydrochloride (Thorazine), he should be given information regarding side-effects
such as

    A. loss of pubic hair and weight gain
    B. agranulocytosis and nausea
    C. gastrointestinal bleeding and gynecomastia
    D. susceptibility to sunburn and potentation of alcohol

17. One day Mr. Tripp remarks to the nurse, Now that I can concentrate move, I can probably 17.____
hold down a job when I'm discharged from the hospital.
Which of these responses by the nurse would probably be MOST appropriate?

    A. Don't you expect to go back to your old job, Mr. Tripp?
    B. You have improved, Mr. Tripp, but you must be careful not to take on too much.
    C. Have you thought of something you might like to do, Mr. Tripp?
    D. There are agencies that will find work for you when you are ready, Mr. Tripp.

Questions 18-25.

DIRECTIONS: Questions 18 through 25 are to be answered on the basis of the following information.

Ms. Nancy Balm, a 20-year-old former music student, is admitted to a psychiatric hospital. Six months after entering school, she was dismissed for engaging in drug parties and sexual orgies in the dormitory. She has also been involved in the theft of a car and in several minor traffic violations. Ms. Balm has grown up in a permissive atmosphere with few controls.

18. After a few days, it is noted that Ms. Balm frequently seeks the attention of one of the female nurses; Ms. Balm calls her by her first name, offers to help her with her work, and frequently tells her that she is the nicest person on the unit.
Based on Ms. Balm's history, it is probably MOST justifiable to say that she

   A. has developed the capacity to be concerned about other people
   B. is asking for help from this nurse
   C. is attempting to use this nurse for her own purposes
   D. genuinely likes this nurse

18.____

19. Ms. Balm is on a locked unit. A new nurse on the unit is about to leave and is holding the key. Ms. Balm approaches, saying eagerly, *Let me turn the key and unlock the door. The other nurses let me.*
Which response by the nurse would be MOST appropriate?

   A. Going to the nurse in charge to ask if Ms. Balm's request should be granted
   B. Telling Ms. Balm in a friendly way that this is not permissible
   C. Letting Ms. Balm turn the key in the lock but keeping close to her while she does it
   D. Asking Ms. Balm why she feels that it is important for her to turn the key

19.____

20. One day Ms. Balm talks with the nurse about the events that led up to her hospitalization. She volunteers the information that she had stolen a car.
Considering the kind of illness she has, which additional comment that she might make would probably BEST indicate her basic attitude?

   A. I wanted a new sportscar, and that one was just what I had been looking for, so I took it.
   B. For a long time, I had wanted to steal a car but had been able to control my desire, but finally it overpowered me.
   C. I knew it was wrong to steal a car, but my friend dared me to.
   D. Once I had driven away in the car, I was sorry I had taken it.

20.____

21. At unit parties, Ms. Balm frequently dances with an elderly man who has chronic brain syndrome. She is courteous to him, though somewhat condescending. The elderly patient receives the attention happily.
It would be CORRECT for staff members to make which of these evaluations about this situation?

   A. Ms. Balm should not be permitted to dance with the elderly patient.
   B. Personnel should let Ms. Balm know that they are aware she is using this means to get approval.
   C. The elderly patient will terminate their relationship if he ceases to obtain pleasure from it.
   D. The activity need not be interrupted as long as both Ms. Balm and the elderly patient receive satisfaction from it.

21.____

22. A young male nurse who works with Ms. Balm has been going to the unit in the evening to see her. When questioned about this, the nurse states that he is fond of Ms. Balm.
It would be ESSENTIAL for the nurse to recognize that

    A. his emotional involvement with Ms. Balm may interfere with his therapeutic effectiveness
    B. Ms. Balm's emotional involvement with him may interfere with her progress
    C. hospital policy prohibits romantic relationships between patients and nurses
    D. Ms. Balm may prove so demanding that he will drop the relationship, thus traumatizing her

23. When Ms. Balm's parents come to see her, they berate her for disgracing them, but they demand special privileges for her from the staff.
It is probably MOST justified to say that they

    A. are unable to express their love directly to their daughter
    B. feel protective toward their daughter
    C. feel that a permissive environment would be better for their daughter
    D. have conflicting feelings about their daughter

24. Several patients are in the dayroom singing with a piano accompaniment. Ms. Balm enters and interrupts the group by turning on the television set. In addition to turning off the television set, which of these responses by the nurse would be MOST appropriate?

    A. Ask Ms. Balm if she would like to lead the group singing.
    B. Tell Ms. Balm that she cannot use the television while the group is singing and offer her a choice of some other activities.
    C. Tell Ms. Balm that she can watch television later.
    D. Tell Ms. Balm that she cannot stay in the dayroom if she continues to disturb the group.

25. Several weeks after Ms. Balm's admission, a group of patients who have written a play for a hospital party ask her to read the script because they know she had a story printed in the hospital newspaper. Ms. Balm agrees to do so and makes several good suggestions to the group, but does not try to assume control of the project.
It is MOST justifiable to say that she is

    A. expressing a need to be liked
    B. indifferent to this project
    C. using a new method of manipulating the group
    D. showing improvement

KEY (CORRECT ANSWERS)

1.	A		11.	C
2.	A		12.	B
3.	C		13.	A
4.	B		14.	A
5.	B		15.	C
6.	D		16.	D
7.	B		17.	C
8.	B		18.	C
9.	A		19.	B
10.	D		20.	A

21. D
22. A
23. D
24. B
25. D

TEST 2

DIRECTIONS: Each question or incomplete statement is followed by several suggested answers or completions. Select the one that BEST answers the question or completes the statement. *PRINT THE LETTER OF THE CORRECT ANSWER IN THE SPACE AT THE RIGHT.*

Questions 1-9.

DIRECTIONS: Questions 1 through 9 are to be answered on the basis of the following information.

Andrew Miles, 18 years old and living away from home for the first time, is a freshman in college. He is admitted to the hospital because he has been having episodes in which he runs about, screams, and then drops to the floor and lies motionless for a few minutes, after which he gets up, mumbles *I'm sorry,* and behaves normally. His school record has been satisfactory, but his contacts with his peer group have decreased greatly because of these episodes. On the basis of diagnostic studies, it has been determined that Mr. Miles' illness is schizophrenia, catatonic type.

1. Stereotyped behavior such as that shown by Mr. Miles can be BEST explained as a(n)

   A. way of assuring predictability
   B. device to gain help and treatment
   C. means of increasing interpersonal distance
   D. attempt to control inner and outer forces

2. The behavior demonstrated by patients such as Mr. Miles is USUALLY thought to be indicative of

   A. damage to the cortex of the brain
   B. an expression of intrapersonal conflict
   C. a deficiency of vitamin B complex in the diet
   D. a disturbance in intellectual functioning

3. Upon Mr. Miles' admission, his needs would BEST be met by a plan that provides

   A. an introduction to each member of the staff
   B. a climate that makes few demands on him
   C. minimal sensory stimulation
   D. time for him to reflect on his problems without interference

4. The day after Mr. Miles' admission, a nurse, Ms. Caan, is assigned to stay with him for a period every day in order to establish a therapeutic nurse-patient relationship.
In carrying out this assignment, it is ESSENTIAL for this nurse to understand that Mr. Miles will probably

   A. be extremely sensitive to the feeling tones of others
   B. be unaware of the nurse's presence
   C. be hostile and verbally abusive
   D. talk if the nurse introduces topics that are of interest to him

5. Which of these insights that Mr. Miles might gain would be MOST basic to his improvement?

   A. Introjection of parental standards in childhood contributed to my personality.
   B. I am a person of worth and value.
   C. My behavior interferes with the development of good relationships.
   D. I require more reassurance than most people do.

6. One day a nurse finds Mr. Miles and another young male patient having an argument in the lounge. The other patient says, *Don't criticize me, you phony. You and your fits!* The other patient is pressing the argument, and Mr. Miles has run behind a chair.
   Which of these measures by the nurse would probably be BEST?

   A. Attempting to find out who started the argument
   B. Firmly directing each patient to go to his room
   C. Engaging the attention of the dominant patient
   D. Explaining to the other patient that Mr. Miles cannot control his spells

7. Mr. Miles now carries on brief conversations with Ms. Caan. During one such conversation, he seems relaxed and affable initially but soon begins to shift his position frequently, grasping the arms of his chair so tightly that his fingers blanch. Ms. Caan remarks to Mr. Miles that he seems tense, to which he replies *Yes*.
   Which of these responses by the nurse at this time would demonstrate the BEST understanding?

   A. I'm beginning to feel tense too, Mr. Miles.
   B. I wonder if I have said something wrong, Mr. Miles.
   C. Do women usually make you feel nervous, Mr. Miles.
   D. At what point in our talk did you begin to feel uneasy, Mr. Miles?

8. When Ms. Caan tells Mr. Miles that she will be off duty for two days, he says flatly, *So what. It doesn't matter.* It is MOST accurate to say that Mr. Miles is

   A. incapable of manifesting emotion
   B. confident of his ability to manage without the nurse
   C. controlling expression of his feelings
   D. apathetic toward the nurse

9. Family therapy is recommended for Mr. Miles. When explaining the purpose of this type of therapy to Mr. Miles' family, which of the following information would it be important to convey to them?

   A. Family members can reinforce the therapist's recommendations between sessions.
   B. Family members need advice in dealing with the identified patient's behavior.
   C. Joint treatment permits equal participation, eliminating anxieties that might otherwise lead to termination of treatment.
   D. Joint treatment alters family interaction, facilitating change in the behavior of the identified patient.

Questions 10-16.

DIRECTIONS: Questions 10 through 16 are to be answered on the basis of the following information.

Fifty-year-old Mr. Jack Dunn, accompanied by his wife, is brought to the emergency room by the police. He has been despondent because he was not promoted in his job. After calling his son to say goodbye, insisting that he was going to end it all, he locked himself in the bathroom, and the police were called to get him out. Mr. Dunn is admitted to the psychiatric unit.

10. Which of these interpretations of Mr. Dunn's behavior should serve as the basis for formulating his nursing care plan?
He

    A. wants to punish those around him
    B. is trying to manipulate his environment
    C. is attempting to get attention and sympathy
    D. is looking for relief from helplessness and hopelessness

11. Which of these statements ACCURATELY assesses Mr. Dunn's potential for suicide?
His

    A. sex and present stress suggest a high risk, but the likelihood of suicide is low in his age group
    B. threat suggests that the risk of suicide is minor
    C. age, sex, and present stress suggest a high risk of suicide
    D. sex suggests a low risk since suicide occurs 30 times more often in females than in males

12. Which of these occurrences would be MOST likely to result in an INCREASE in Mr. Dunn's suicidal thoughts?
His

    A. expressing hostility overtly before he is able to tolerate doing so
    B. entrance into a deeply retarded phase of depression
    C. being required to perform work in the kitchen
    D. being allowed to talk about his morbid ideas

13. During a staff conference concerning Mr. Dunn's care, a young nursing student says, *Even though I know that* Mr. Dunn's condition requires time to respond to therapy, I feel discouraged when I'm with him. No matter what I do, he talks about his failures and makes no attempt to help himself.
The interpretation of the student's reaction to Mr. Dunn's behavior that is probably MOST justifiable is that the

    A. student's difficulty arises from an attitude of hopelessness toward older persons
    B. student feels that Mr. Dunn's condition is not remediable unless he is willing to help himself
    C. student has set up a failure situation that is detrimental to therapeutic usefulness to Mr. Dunn
    D. student's self-concept as a helping person is being threatened

14. A nurse finds Mr. Dunn cutting his wrist with a razor blade.
    Which of these actions should the nurse take?

    A. Shout *Stop!* and then say, *Tell me what caused your despair.*
    B. Say, *Think of what it would do to your family!*
    C. Grab Mr. Dunn's arm to stop him and say, *I'm going to stay with you.*
    D. Say, *Why, Mr. Dunn! You've just begun to feel better and now look what you've done.*

15. Mr. Dunn seems improved and is sent home on a trial visit. He is then admitted to the intensive care unit for treatment for a self-inflicted gunshot wound in the chest. When he is somewhat improved, Mr. Dunn remarks, *Everyone here must think I'm some kind of freak.*
    Which of these responses would be MOST appropriate?

    A. *None of us thinks that you are a freak.*
    B. *You feel that others are judging you.*
    C. *I understand that you were upset when this happened.*
    D. *What made you so desperate that you did a thing like this?*

16. Mr. Dunn has improved and is discharged. A few days after Mr. Dunn returns to work, while he is talking with a co-worker, a number of things go wrong in the office. Mr. Dunn slams a book on the table and says, *Dammit!* The co-worker who is present is aware that Mr. Dunn has been mentally ill.
    Which of these actions on the part of the co-worker would be BEST?

    A. Wait for Mr. Dunn to cool off and then resume the discussion.
    B. Suggest that Mr. Dunn go home and remain there until he calms down.
    C. Urge Mr. Dunn to take his tranquilizers.
    D. Talk with Mr. Dunn about his particular need for controlling outbursts.

Questions 17-25.

DIRECTIONS: Questions 17 through 25 are to be answered on the basis of the following information.

Ms. Julia Warren, 53 years old and with no previous history of mental illness, is admitted to a private psychiatric hospital because of symptoms, including pacing, wringing her hands, moaning, beating her forehead, and saying, *I'm a terrible woman.* She has been unable to do her job as a bookkeeper and has had to have members of her family stay with her day and night.

17. The extent of the nurse's orientation of Ms. Warren to the hospital environment should be based CHIEFLY upon Ms. Warren's

    A. willingness to stay with the nurse
    B. ability to concentrate
    C. persistence in making demands on other patients
    D. acceptance of the need for hospitalization

18. During the acute phase of Ms. Warren's illness, it is ESSENTIAL that the nurse have the ability to

   A. minimize stimuli in Ms. Warren's environment
   B. interest Ms. Warren in a variety of activities
   C. accept Ms. Warren's self-accusations
   D. strengthen Ms. Warren's intellectual defenses

18.____

19. Ms. Warren shows typical distress upon being informed of her impending electric convulsive therapy. Which understanding by the nurse would BEST serve as the basis for preparing Ms. Warren psychologically for it?

   A. Misinformation may be contributing to her anxiety.
   B. Emphasizing the safety of the procedure will reduce her fear.
   C. Knowing that most people have the same response is usually comforting.
   D. A high level of anxiety renders an individual more receptive to information given by helping persons.

19.____

20. Depressions of the type Ms. Warren has usually respond well to electric convulsive therapy, but the consequent memory loss is quite disturbing.
The nurse can be MOST helpful to the patient who has such a loss of memory by

   A. engaging the patient in diversional activities
   B. reporting the problem to the physician
   C. explaining to the patient that other patients receiving this therapy also have this problem
   D. reassuring the patient repeatedly that this is an expected and temporary reaction

20.____

21. Which of the following defense mechanisms is MOST likely to be used by a person who is as depressed as Ms. Warren?

   A. Turning against the self
   B. Projection
   C. Rationalization
   D. Displacement of instinctual aims

21.____

22. When Ms. Warren learns that occupational therapy has been ordered for her, she scoffs at the idea, saying it is silly.
If Ms. Warren were to think all of the following thoughts regarding occupational therapy, which one would be MOST acceptable to her?

   A. This is enjoyable.
   B. I'm helping to pay for my care.
   C. This keeps me from thinking about my failures.
   D. I didn't know that I was so creative,

22.____

23. Ms. Warren is assigned to group therapy. Which of these ideas would it be MOST desirable for each participant to gain?

   A. Each person's opinion is respected.
   B. Verbalization will help each individual to gain insight.
   C. Each member has a responsibility to other members of the group.
   D. The group work consists of analyzing each other's motivations.

23.____

24. Ms. Warren improves and goes out with her husband for the afternoon. That evening, a nurse finds Ms. Warren sitting by herself in the dayroom.
Which of these comments by the nurse would probably be BEST?

    A. Why are you so preoccupied, Ms. Warren?
    B. You look tired, Ms. Warren. Was your afternoon too much for you?
    C. You seem very quiet, Ms. Warren.
    D. You looked happier yesterday, Ms. Warren.

24.____

25. Ms. Warren is discharged. The day Ms. Warren goes back to work, Bob, a customer she has known for many years, comes in and says, *Hello there, Julia. Good to see you back! your boss told me that you were sick. What was wrong with you?* Which of these replies by Ms. Warren would indicate that she accepted her illness and has recovered?

    A. I was kind of mixed up for a while, Bob, but I'm all right now.
    B. I just didn't feel good, Bob. Old age coming on, I guess.
    C. I was just down in the dumps, Bob, but my doctor insisted that I go to the hospital. You know how they are.
    D. I'm glad to be back. What can I do for you, Bob?

25.____

KEY (CORRECT ANSWERS)

1.	D		11.	C
2.	B		12.	A
3.	B		13.	D
4.	A		14.	C
5.	B		15.	B
6.	C		16.	A
7.	D		17.	B
8.	C		18.	C
9.	D		19.	A
10.	D		20.	D

21. A
22. B
23. A
24. C
25. A

TEST 3

DIRECTIONS: Each question or incomplete statement is followed by several suggested answers or completions. Select the one that BEST answers the question or completes the statement. *PRINT THE LETTER OF THE CORRECT ANSWER IN THE SPACE AT THE RIGHT.*

Questions 1-7.

DIRECTIONS: Questions 1 through 7 are to be answered on the basis of the following information.

When Mark Levine, 5 1/2 years old, goes to school for the first time, he screams and seems terrified when he sees the drinking fountain near his classroom door. Mark's mother tells the school nurse that he has an intense fear of drinking fountains.

1. The understanding of Mark's fear of fountains that is MOST justifiable is that it 1.____
    A. is a symptom common in dyslexic children
    B. is not subject to his conscious control
    C. stems from his lack of understanding of plumbing
    D. results from having learned that his symptoms have a manipulative potential

2. Behavior therapy will be used in treating Mark's symptoms. His plan of care will include 2.____
    A. authoritative instruction
    B. increased cultural orientation
    C. direct interpretations
    D. systematic desensitization

3. Mark's behavior reflects his need to control anxiety by 3.____
    A. refusing to recognize the source of his anxiety
    B. making a conscious effort to avoid situations that cause anxiety
    C. substituting a neutral object as the target of his negative feelings
    D. acting in a manner opposite to his underlying need

4. Parents should be instructed that a child's mental health will BEST be promoted if the love he receives from his parents 4.____
    A. is related to the child's behavior
    B. is unconditional
    C. makes externally imposed discipline unnecessary
    D. is reinforced by unchanging physical demonstrations

5. Ms. Levine calls the community mental health clinic and tells the nurse that Mark has suddenly become terrified of getting into the family car, refuses to do so, and is in the yard screaming uncontrollably. 5.____
What would it be BEST for the nurse to tell Ms. Levine to do FIRST?
    A. Hold Mark snugly and talk softly to him.
    B. Give Mark a warm bath and put him to bed.
    C. Bring Mark to the clinic as soon as possible.
    D. Remind Mark that he has never before been afraid of automobiles.

6. Mark is having play therapy.
The choice of play therapy for children of Mark's age should PROBABLY be based upon their inability to

   A. overcome inhibitors about revealing family conflicts and behaviors
   B. differentiate between reality and fantasy
   C. recognize the difference between right and wrong
   D. adequately describe feelings and experience

7. On a rainy day, after Mark's play-therapy session, Ms. Levine hands Mark his overshoes and says, *Put them on. It's pouring outside.* Mark answers defiantly, *No, they're too hard to put on. I can't.* Then he sits down on a bench and pouts. Ms. Levine looks at the nurse in a perplexed way, saying nothing.
Which of these responses by the nurse would probably be BEST?

   A. Say to Ms. Levine, *Maybe the overshoes are too small to Mark.*
   B. Sit on the bench with Mark and say calmly, *It's raining. You start pulling your overshoes on, and I'll help you with the hard part.*
   C. Hand Mark his overshoes and say to him in a matter-of-fact way, *If you will put the first one one, I'll put on the second one for you.*
   D. Say to Mark, firmly but kindly, *You are trying to test your mother's authority. This behavior will not be tolerated. Put your overshoes on right now.*

Questions 8-14.

DIRECTIONS: Questions 8 through 14 are to be answered on the basis of the following information.

Ms. Eileen Gray, 33 years old, is admitted to the psychiatric hospital with a diagnosis of obsessive-compulsive reaction. Her chief fear is that her excreta may harm others on the unit. As a result, she spends hours in the bathroom washing not only her hands, arms, vulva, and anal area, but also the walls, toilet, and toilet stall. In the process, she discards wet paper towels in every direction and leaves puddles of water everywhere.

8. Ms. Gray's symptoms are MOST clearly an example of

   A. sublimation of anxiety-producing fantasies and daydreams
   B. compensation for an imaginary object loss
   C. a symbolic expression of conflict and guilt feelings
   D. an infantile maneuver to avoid intimacy

9. On the unit, Ms. Gray carries out her elaborate washing routine several times a day. She says to the nurse, *I guess all this seems awfully silly to you.*
It is MOST justifiable to say that she

   A. is asking the nurse to keep her from performing these unreasonable acts
   B. really believes her acts are completely rational, and she is testing the nurse
   C. is indicating an appreciation of the unreasonable-ness of her behavior
   D. is deliberately putting the nurse in a difficult position

10. The nurse should understand that the probable effect of permitting Ms. Gray to perform her washing routines will be to

   A. confirm a basic delusion
   B. help Ms. Gray to perceive how illogical her behavior is
   C. create distrust of the nurse, who ought to symbolize reality
   D. temporarily reduce Ms. Gray's anxiety

11. Ms. Gray is unable to get to the dining room in time for breakfast because of her washing rituals.
During the early period of her hospitalization, it would be MOST appropriate to

   A. wake Ms. Gray early enough so that she can perform her rituals in time to get to breakfast
   B. firmly insist that Ms. Gray interrupt her rituals at breakfast time
   C. explain to Ms. Gray that her rituals are not helping her to get well
   D. give Ms. Gray a choice between completing her rituals or going to breakfast

12. During a nursing team conference, staff members voice frustration concerning Ms. Gray's constant questions such as *Shall I go to lunch or finish cleaning my room?* and *Should I go to O.T. or mend my coat?*
In order to deal effectively with this behavior, team members should know that Ms. Gray's

   A. dependence upon staff is a symptom that needs to be interrupted by firm limit-setting
   B. inability to make decisions reflects her basic anxiety about failure
   C. indecisiveness is meant to test the staff's acceptance of her
   D. relentless need to seek attention represents a developmental arrest at the autistic (prototaxic) level

13. Ms. Gray is being treated by psychotherapy. The physician tells the nurse to expect her to be upset at times when she returns from her session with him and to let her be upset.
By this directive, the physician MOST probably wants to

   A. put Ms. Gray under stress so that she will become more responsive to suggestions
   B. teach Ms. Gray to be satisfied with advice from only one person
   C. help Ms. Gray become aware of her feelings
   D. make Ms. Gray independent, which would not be possible if she were to develop alliances with members of the nursing staff

14. Ms. Gray is given her first pass to spend the night at home. As the time approaches for her to leave the hospital, she seems increasingly tense and says, *Maybe I shouldn't stay home all night. Maybe I should just stay for dinner and then come back here.* When the nurse responds nondirectively, Ms. Gray answers, *I'm just sort of anxious about things in general. It's nothing specific.*
Which of these responses by the nurse would probably be BEST?

   A. Everyone is scared of his first overnight pass. You'll find that it will be easier than you expect.
   B. It's understandable that you are concerned about your first night at home. Would it help if you make the decision after you've been home for a while and see how things are going?

4 (#3)

  C. I know how you feel, but the staff think that you are well enough to stay home overnight. Won't you try to do so?
  D. It's important for you to try to remain at home overnight. If you are able to do it, it will be a measure of your improvement.

Questions 15-25.

DIRECTIONS: Questions 15 through 25 are to be answered on the basis of the following information.

Ms. Kathy Collins, 47 years old, has been hospitalized several times over a period of years because of episodes of elation and depression. She lives with her mother and sister. She is well known to the nursing staff. While she is again being admitted, she is chainsmoking cigarettes, walking back and forth, and talking loudly and gaily about her romantic successes.

15. Which of these greetings by the nurse who is admitting Ms. Collins would probably be MOST appropriate?

  A. We're sorry you had to come back, Ms. Collins, but we are glad to see you.
  B. Good morning, Ms. Collins. Your doctor called to say you were coming. I will show you to your room.
  C. Hello, Ms. Collins. You're cheerful this morning.
  D. It's good to see you again, Ms. Collins. You don't seem to mind coming back to the hospital.

16. The nurse who will care for Ms. Collins each day should expect to make use of which of these interventions?

  A. Distracting and redirecting
  B. Orienting and reminding
  C. Explaining and praising
  D. Evoking anger and encouraging insight

17. Ms. Collins is an overactive patient with a mood disturbance rather than a thought disorder.
Because of this type of illness, the nursing care plan should include measures that respond to the fact that she is

  A. disoriented
  B. easily stimulated by what is going on around her
  C. preoccupied with a single idea
  D. likely to be panicked by physical contact

18. Which of these nursing goals is likely to require the MOST attention while Ms. Collins is acutely ill?

  A. Orientation to time, place, and person
  B. Establishment of a sense of self-esteem
  C. Promotion of adequate rest
  D. Prevention of circulatory stasis

19. Ms. Collins and her roommate are in their room. While passing by, a registered nurse hears them arguing. Ms. Collins says, *You're a slob. How can anybody live in this mess!* The roommate answers, *What right do you have to say that?* and starts to cry.
Which of these interventions by the nurse would be appropriate?

    A. Enter the room and say to Ms. Collins, *You have upset your roommate. She's crying.*
    B. Enter and say, *It sounds as if you are both upset.*
    C. Stand in the doorway and say, *It's part of your therapy to learn how to get along together.*
    D. Take the roommate aside and explain to her that Ms. Collins can be expected to be difficult for a few days.

19.____

20. Ms. Collins is not eating sufficient food. Which approach by the nurse would probably be BEST as a first step in trying to get her to eat more?

    A. Giving her foods that she can eat with her fingers while she is moving about
    B. Conveying to her tactfully the idea that she has to eat
    C. Serving her food to her on a tray and telling her firmly but kindly to eat
    D. Assuring her that she can have anything she wants to eat whenever she wants it

20.____

21. The physician orders lithium carbonate for Ms. Collins. To accompany the order for lithium carbonate, the physician is likely to specify that

    A. the patient should lie down for a half hour after each dose
    B. the medication should be evenly distributed throughout each 24-hour period
    C. a salt-free diet should be provided for the patient
    D. the drug level of the patient's blood should be monitored regularly

21.____

22. When their desires are frustrated, patients such as Ms. Collins are likely to

    A. maintain a superficial affability
    B. sulk and retire temporarily from the situation
    C. suddenly show hostility and aggression
    D. seek support from personnel

22.____

23. Group psychotherapy is ordered for Ms. Collins. The CHIEF purpose of this therapy is to help her to

    A. socialize easily with a group
    B. gain self-knowledge through the sharing of problems
    C. identify various types of emotional problems and ways in which people handle them
    D. become acquainted with types of problems that will be encountered after discharge

23.____

24. After several days, Ms. Collins' behavior changes, and she becomes depressed. One night the nurse finds Ms. Collins unconscious in bed with a strip of her sheet tied around her neck. She is cyanotic and her respirations are labored and stertorous. After loosening the constriction around Ms. Collins' neck and signaling for help, which of these actions by the nurse would demonstrate the BEST judgment?

    A. Remain with her.
    B. Place her in the proper position and start artificial respiration.

24.____

C. Give her a vigorous thump on the sternum.
D. Raise the foot of her bed.

25. Ms. Collins is gradually improving, and the team talks of plans for her discharge. On a visit to the unit, Ms. Collins' mother and sister tell the nurse that Ms. Collins doesn't seem much better, and they are very hesitant about having her return home because of the previous problems they've had with her. Which of these actions should INITIALLY be taken by the nurse?

25.____

A. Suggest that the family find a place where Ms. Collins can live by herself after discharge.
B. Elaborate on Ms. Collins' hospital regimen and the normality of her present behavior.
C. Assure the relatives that Ms. Collins is better and refer them to the physician if they have further questions.
D. Listen to Ms. Collins' relatives and suggest that they make an appointment with the family counselor.

KEY (CORRECT ANSWERS)

1.	B	11.	A
2.	D	12.	B
3.	C	13.	C
4.	B	14.	B
5.	A	15.	B
6.	D	16.	A
7.	B	17.	B
8.	C	18.	C
9.	C	19.	B
10.	D	20.	A

21.	D
22.	C
23.	B
24.	A
25.	D

CPSIA information can be obtained
at www.ICGtesting.com
Printed in the USA
LVHW060200201120
672237LV00033B/209

9 781731 841988